Laboratory Activities

Glencoe Science

TEKS Edition

Texas Science

GRADE 7

NATIONAL GEOGRAPHIC SOCIETY

tx.science.glencoe.com

Glencoe McGraw-Hill

New York, New York   Columbus, Ohio   Woodland Hills, California   Peoria, Illinois

Glencoe Science

Student Edition
Teacher Wraparound Edition
Interactive Teacher Edition CD-ROM
Interactive Lesson Planner CD-ROM
Lesson Plans
Content Outline for Teaching
Dinah Zike's Teaching Science with Foldables
Directed Reading for Content Mastery
Foldables: Reading and Study Skills
Assessment
   Chapter Review
   Chapter Tests
   ExamView Pro Test Bank Software
   Assessment Transparencies
   Performance Assessment in the Science
     Classroom
   The Princeton Review Standardized Test
     Practice Booklet
Directed Reading for Content Mastery in Spanish
Spanish Resources
English/Spanish Guided Reading Audio Program

Reinforcement
Enrichment
Activity Worksheets
Section Focus Transparencies
Teaching Transparencies
Laboratory Activities
Science Inquiry Labs
Critical Thinking/Problem Solving
Reading and Writing Skill Activities
Mathematics Skill Activities
Cultural Diversity
Laboratory Management and Safety in the Science
   Classroom
MindJogger Videoquizzes and Teacher Guide
Interactive Explorations and Quizzes CD-ROM
Vocabulary Puzzlemaker Software
Cooperative Learning in the Science Classroom
Environmental Issues in the Science Classroom
Home and Community Involvement
Using the Internet in the Science Classroom

Answers to the worksheets on pages vii-xi can be found on page 24
of Laboratory Management and Safety in the Science Classroom.

Glencoe/McGraw-Hill

A Division of The McGraw·Hill Companies

Send all inquiries to:
Glencoe/McGraw-Hill
8787 Orion Place
Columbus, OH 43240

ISBN 0-07-825499-X
Printed in the United States of America
4 5 6 7 8 9 10 009 06 05 04 03

Table of Contents

Getting Started v
Laboratory Equipment vii
SI Reference Sheet xiii
Safety Symbols xv
Student Laboratory and Safety Guidelines xvi
Student Science Laboratory Safety Contract xvii

Chapter 1   The Nature of Science
    1   A Scientific Method 1
    2   Using a Scientific Method 3

Chapter 2   Earth in Space
    1   Getting Close to the Moon 7
    2   Building a Sundial 11

Chapter 3   Matter
    1   Mixtures and Compounds 15
    2   Constructing Compounds 17

Chapter 4   Properties and Changes of Matter
    1   Comparing Viscosity 19
    2   Chemical Changes 23

Chapter 5   Motion, Forces, and Simple Machines
    1   Speed of Falling Objects 27
    2   Newton's First Law of Motion 31

Chapter 6   Energy
    1   Radiation 33
    2   Chemical Potential Energy—You Are What You Eat! 37

Chapter 7   Bacteria, Protists, and Fungi
    1   Shapes of Bacteria 39
    2   Molds 41

Chapter 8   Invertebrate Animals
    1   Earthworm Anatomy 43
    2   Grasshopper Anatomy 47

Chapter 9   Vertebrate Animals
    1   Fish Dissection 51
    2   Owl Pellets 55

Chapter 10   Plants
    1   Root Structure and Functions 57
    2   Parts of a Fruit 59

Chapter 11   Plant Processes
    1   Water Loss 61
    2   Tropisms 63

Chapter 12   Cell Reproduction
1   Modeling Cell Division in Early Development 67
2   Examining Models of Chromosomes 69

Chapter 13   Heredity
1   Genetic Traits 73
2   50:50 Chances 75

Chapter 14   Circulation and Immunity
1   Heart Structure 77
2   Blood Pressure 81

Chapter 15   Respiration and Excretion
1   How does breathing occur? 85
2   Lung Capacity 89

Chapter 16   Nutrients and Digestion
1   Testing for Carbohydrates 91
2   Digestion of Fats 95

Chapter 17   Structure and Movement
1   Analyzing Bones 99
2   Muscle Action 103

Chapter 18   Control and Coordination
1   Which brain side is dominant? 107
2   Parts of the Eye 111

Chapter 19   Regulation and Reproduction
1   The Effects of Epinephrine on a Planarian 115
2   Fetal Development 119

Chapter 20   Interactions of Life
1   Communities 121
2   Changes in Predator and Prey Populations 125

Chapter 21   Ecosystems
1   Succession Communities and Grasses 129
2   Exploring Life in Pond Water 131

Chapter 22   Conserving Resources
1   Water Pollution 135
2   What to Do with Plastic 139

Chapter 23   Weathering and Soil
1   Chemical Weathering 143
2   Soil Infiltration by Groundwater 145

Chapter 24   Erosional Forces
1   Mass Movements 147
2   Modeling a Glacier 149

Chapter 25   Water Erosion and Deposition
1   Capillary Action 151
2   Carbon Dioxide and Limestone 153

Getting Started

Science is the body of information including all the hypotheses and experiments that tell us about our environment. All people involved in scientific work use similar methods for gaining information. One important scientific skill is the ability to obtain data directly from the environment. Observations must be based on what actually happens in the environment. Equally important is the ability to organize these data into a form from which valid conclusions can be drawn. These conclusions must be such that other scientists can achieve the same results in the laboratory.

To make the most of your laboratory experience, you need to continually work to increase your laboratory skills. These skills include the ability to recognize and use equipment properly and to measure and use SI units accurately. Safety also must be an ongoing concern. To help you get started in discovering many fascinating things about the world around you, the next few pages provide you with:

- a visual overview of basic **laboratory equipment** for you to label
- a reference sheet of **SI units**
- a reference sheet of **safety symbols**
- a list of your **safety responsibilities** in the laboratory
- a **safety contract**

Each lab activity in this manual includes the following sections:
- an investigation **title** and introductory section providing information about the problem under study
- a **strategy** section identifying the **objective(s)** of the activity
- a list of needed **materials**
- safety concerns identified with **safety icons** and **caution statements**
- a set of step-by-step **procedures**
- a section to help you record your **data and observations**
- a section to help you **analyze your data** and record your **conclusions**
- a closing **strategy check** so that you can review your achievement of the objectives of the activity

Laboratory Equipment

Figure 1

1. _____

2. _____

3. _____

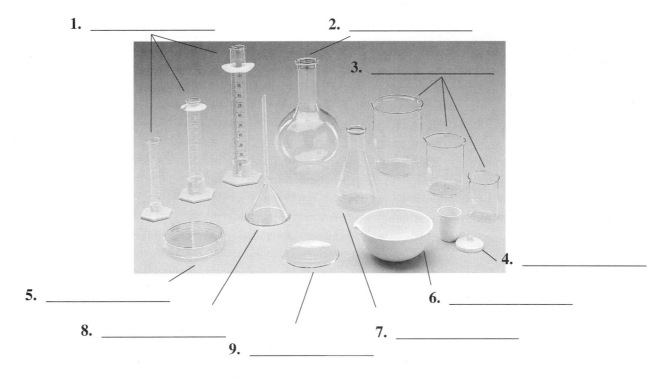

4. _____

5. _____

6. _____

7. _____

8. _____

9. _____

Figure 2

1. _____

3. _____

2. _____

4. _____

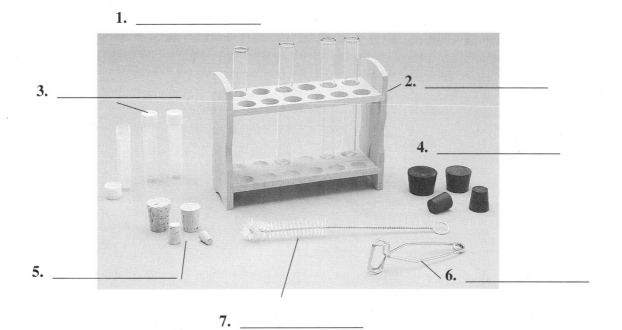

5. _____

6. _____

7. _____

Laboratory Equipment (continued)

Figure 3

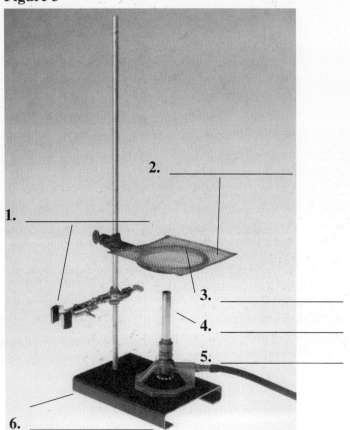

1. _____
2. _____
3. _____
4. _____
5. _____
6. _____

Figure 4

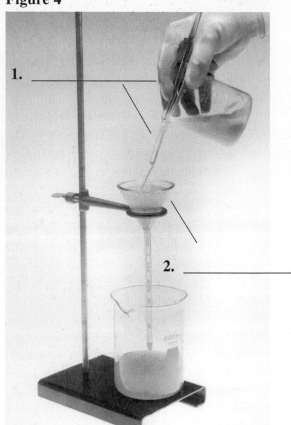

1. _____
2. _____

Figure 5

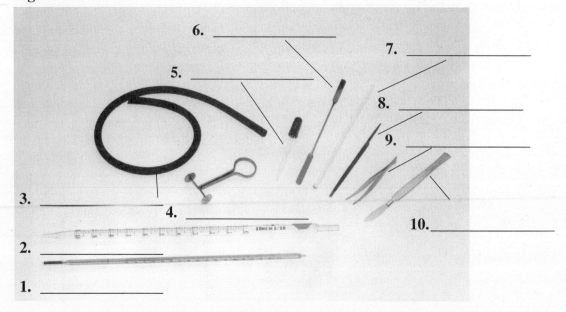

1. _____
2. _____
3. _____
4. _____
5. _____
6. _____
7. _____
8. _____
9. _____
10. _____

Laboratory Equipment (continued)

Figure 6

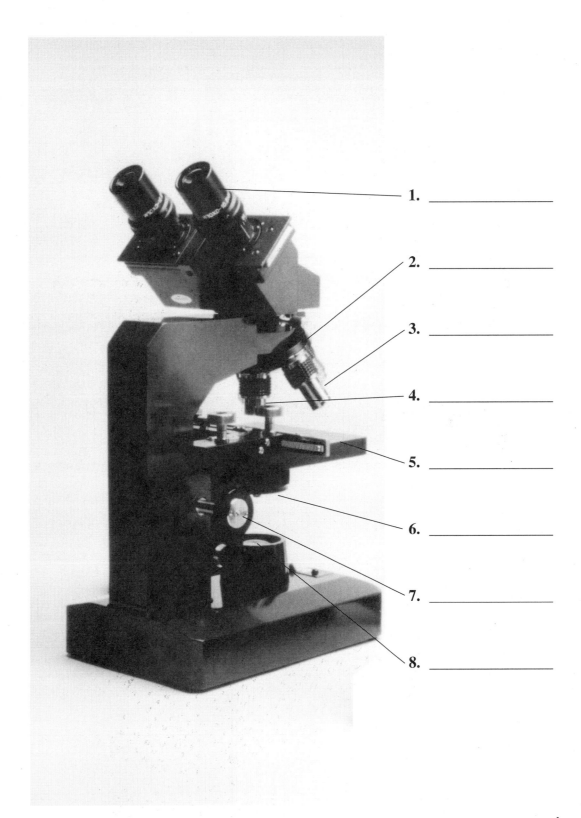

1. _____

2. _____

3. _____

4. _____

5. _____

6. _____

7. _____

8. _____

Laboratory Equipment (continued)

Figure 7

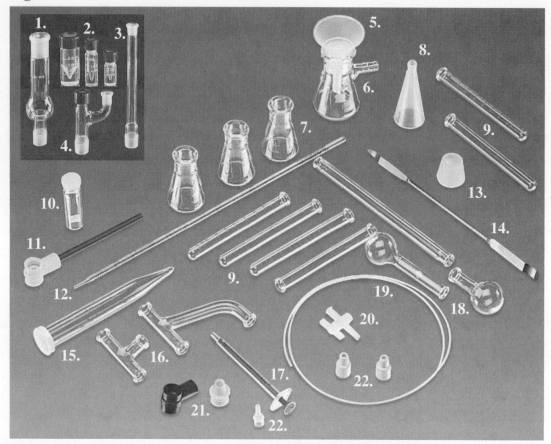

1. _____
2. _____
3. _____
4. _____
5. _____
6. _____
7. _____
8. _____
9. _____
10. _____
11. _____

12. _____
13. _____
14. _____
15. _____
16. _____
17. _____
18. _____
19. _____
20. _____
21. _____
22. _____

Laboratory Equipment (continued)

Figure 8

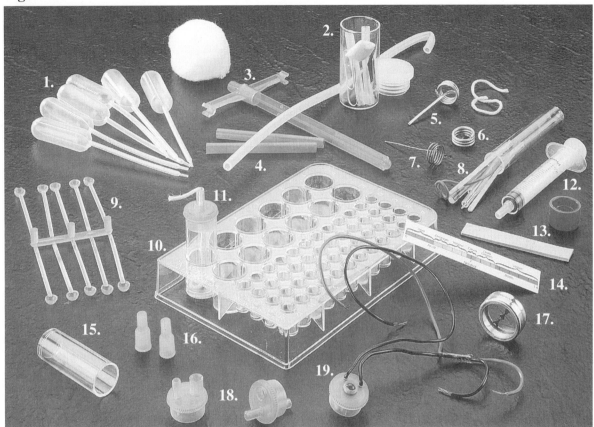

1. _____
2. _____
3. _____
4. _____
5. _____
6. _____
7. _____
8. _____
9. _____
10. _____

11. _____
12. _____
13. _____
14. _____
15. _____
16. _____
17. _____
18. _____
19. _____

SI Reference Sheet

The International System of Units (SI) is accepted as the standard for measurement throughout most of the world. Frequently used SI units are listed in **Table 1** and some supplementary SI units in **Table 2.**

Table 1

Frequently Used SI Units	
Length	1 millimeter (mm) = 100 micrometers (μm) 1 centimeter (cm) = 10 millimeters (mm) 1 meter (m) = 100 centimeters (cm) 1 kilometer (km) = 1,000 meters (m) 1 light-year = 9,460,000,000,000 kilometers (km)
Area	1 square meter (m^2) = 10,000 square centimeters (cm^2) 1 square kilometer (km^2) = 1,000,000 square meters (m^2)
Volume	1 milliliter (mL) = 1 cubic centimeter (cm^3) 1 liter (L) = 1,000 milliliters (mL)
Mass	1 gram (g) = 1,000 milligrams (mg) 1 kilogram (kg) = 1,000 grams (g) 1 metric ton = 1,000 kilograms (kg)
Time	1 s = 1 second

Table 2

Supplementary SI Units			
Measurement	**Unit**	**Symbol**	**Expressed in base units**
Energy	joule	J	$kg \cdot m^2/s^2$
Force	newton	N	$kg \cdot m/s^2$
Power	watt	W	$kg \cdot m^2/s^3$ or J/s
Pressure	pascal	Pa	$kg/m \cdot s^2$ or $N \cdot m$

Sometimes quantities are measured using different SI units. In order to use them together in an equation, you must convert all of the quantities into the same unit. To convert, you multiply by a conversion factor. A conversion factor is a ratio that is equal to one. Make a conversion factor by building a ratio of equivalent units. Place the new units in the numerator and the old units in the denominator. For example, to convert 1.255 L to mL, multiply 1.255 L by the appropriate ratio as follows:

$$1.255 \text{ L} \times 1,000 \text{ mL}/1 \text{ L} = 1,255 \text{ mL}$$

The unit L cancels just as if it were a number.

Temperature measurements in SI often are made in degrees Celsius. Celsius temperature is a supplementary unit derived from the base unit kelvin. The Celsius scale (°C) has 100 equal graduations between the freezing temperature (0°C) and the boiling temperature of water (100°C). The following relationship exists between the Celsius and kelvin temperature scales:

$$K = °C + 273$$

SI Reference Sheet (continued)

To convert from °F to °C, you can:

1. For exact amounts, use the equation at the bottom of **Table 3**, or
2. For approximate amounts, find °F on the thermometer at the left of **Figure 1** and determine °C on the thermometer at the right.

Table 3

Figure 1

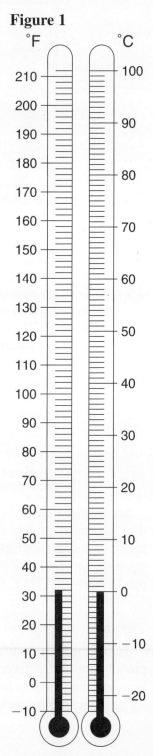

SI Metric to English Conversions			
	When you have:	**Multiply by:**	**To find:**
Length	inches	2.54	centimeters
	centimeters	0.39	inches
	feet	0.30	meters
	meters	3.28	feet
	yards	0.91	meters
	meters	1.09	yards
	miles	1.61	kilometers
	kilometers	0.62	miles
Mass and weight*	ounces	28.35	grams
	grams	0.04	ounces
	pounds	0.45	kilograms
	kilograms	2.20	pounds
	tons	0.91	metric tons
	metric tons	1.10	tons
	pounds	4.45	newtons
	newtons	0.23	pounds
Volume	cubic inches	16.39	cubic centimeters
	milliliters	0.06	cubic inches
	cubic feet	0.03	cubic meters
	cubic meters	35.31	cubic feet
	liters	1.06	quarts
	liters	0.26	gallons
	gallons	3.78	liters
Area	square inches	6.45	square centimeters
	square centimeters	0.16	square inches
	square feet	0.09	square meters
	square meters	10.76	square feet
	square miles	2.59	square kilometers
	square kilometers	0.39	square miles
	hectares	2.47	acres
	acres	0.40	hectares
Temperature	Fahrenheit	$\frac{5}{9}(°F - 32)$	Celsius
	Celsius	$\frac{9}{5}°C + 32$	Fahrenheit

* Weight as measured in standard Earth gravity

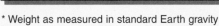

SAFETY SYMBOLS

	HAZARD	EXAMPLES	PRECAUTION	REMEDY
DISPOSAL	Special disposal procedures need to be followed.	certain chemicals, living organisms	Do not dispose of these materials in the sink or trash can.	Dispose of wastes as directed by your teacher.
BIOLOGICAL	Organisms or other biological materials that might be harmful to humans	bacteria, fungi, blood, unpreserved tissues, plant materials	Avoid skin contact with these materials. Wear mask or gloves.	Notify your teacher if you suspect contact with material. Wash hands thoroughly.
EXTREME TEMPERATURE	Objects that can burn skin by being too cold or too hot	boiling liquids, hot plates, dry ice, liquid nitrogen	Use proper protection when handling.	Go to your teacher for first aid.
SHARP OBJECT	Use of tools or glassware that can easily puncture or slice skin	razor blades, pins, scalpels, pointed tools, dissecting probes, broken glass	Practice common-sense behavior and follow guidelines for use of the tool.	Go to your teacher for first aid.
FUME	Possible danger to respiratory tract from fumes	ammonia, acetone, nail polish remover, heated sulfur, moth balls	Make sure there is good ventilation. Never smell fumes directly. Wear a mask.	Leave foul area and notify your teacher immediately.
ELECTRICAL	Possible danger from electrical shock or burn	improper grounding, liquid spills, short circuits, exposed wires	Double-check setup with teacher. Check condition of wires and apparatus.	Do not attempt to fix electrical problems. Notify your teacher immediately.
IRRITANT	Substances that can irritate the skin or mucus membranes of the respiratory tract	pollen, moth balls, steel wool, fiber glass, potassium permanganate	Wear dust mask and gloves. Practice extra care when handling these materials.	Go to your teacher for first aid.
CHEMICAL	Chemicals that can react with and destroy tissue and other materials	bleaches such as hydrogen peroxide; acids such as sulfuric acid, hydrochloric acid; bases such as ammonia, sodium hydroxide	Wear goggles, gloves, and an apron.	Immediately flush the affected area with water and notify your teacher.
TOXIC	Substance may be poisonous if touched, inhaled, or swallowed	mercury, many metal compounds, iodine, poinsettia plant parts	Follow your teacher's instructions.	Always wash hands thoroughly after use. Go to your teacher for first aid.
OPEN FLAME	Open flame may ignite flammable chemicals, loose clothing, or hair	alcohol, kerosene, potassium permanganate, hair, clothing	Tie back hair. Avoid wearing loose clothing. Avoid open flames when using flammable chemicals. Be aware of locations of fire safety equipment.	Notify your teacher immediately. Use fire safety equipment if applicable.

 Eye Safety Proper eye protection should be worn at all times by anyone performing or observing science activities.

 Clothing Protection This symbol appears when substances could stain or burn clothing.

 Animal Safety This symbol appears when safety of animals and students must be ensured.

 Radioactivity This symbol appears when radioactive materials are used.

Student Laboratory and Safety Guidelines

Regarding Emergencies

- Inform the teacher immediately of *any* mishap—fire, injury, glassware breakage, chemical spills, and so forth.
- Follow your teacher's instructions and your school's procedures in dealing with emergencies.

Regarding Your Person

- Do NOT wear clothing that is loose enough to catch on anything and avoid sandals or open-toed shoes.
- Wear protective safety gloves, goggles, and aprons as instructed.
- Always wear safety goggles (not glasses) when using hazardous chemicals.
- Wear goggles throughout entire activity, cleanup, and handwashing.
- Keep your hands away from your face while working in the laboratory.
- Remove synthetic fingernails before working in the lab (these are highly flammable).
- Do NOT use hair spray, mousse, or other flammable hair products just before or during laboratory work where an open flame is used (they can ignite easily).
- Tie back long hair and loose clothing to keep them away from flames and equipment.
- Remove loose jewelry—chains or bracelets—while doing lab work.
- NEVER eat or drink while in the lab or store food in lab equipment or the lab refrigerator.
- Do NOT inhale vapors or taste, touch, or smell any chemical or substance unless instructed to do so by your teacher.

Regarding Your Work

- Read all instructions before you begin a laboratory or field activity. Ask questions if you do not understand any part of the activity.
- Work ONLY on activities assigned by your teacher.
- Do NOT substitute other chemicals/substances for those listed in your activity.
- Do NOT begin any activity until directed to do so by your teacher.
- Do NOT handle any equipment without specific permission.
- Remain in your own work area unless given permission by your teacher to leave it.
- Do NOT point heated containers—test tubes, flasks, and so forth—at yourself or anyone else.
- Do NOT take any materials or chemicals out of the classroom.
- Stay out of storage areas unless you are instructed to be there and are supervised by your teacher.
- NEVER work alone in the laboratory.
- When using dissection equipment, always cut away from yourself and others. Cut downward, never stabbing at the object.
- Handle living organisms or preserved specimens only when authorized by your teacher.
- Always wear heavy gloves when handling animals. If you are bitten or stung, notify your teacher immediately.

Regarding Cleanup

- Keep work and lab areas clean, limiting the amount of easily ignitable materials.
- Turn off all burners and other equipment before leaving the lab.
- Carefully dispose of waste materials as instructed by your teacher.
- Wash your hands thoroughly with soap and warm water after each activity.

Student Science Laboratory Safety Contract

I agree to:

- Act responsibly at all times in the laboratory.
- Follow all instructions given, orally or in writing, by my teacher.
- Perform only those activities assigned and approved by my teacher.
- Protect my eyes, face, hands, and body by wearing proper clothing and using protective equipment provided by my school.
- Carry out good housekeeping practices as instructed by my teacher.
- Know the location of safety and first aid equipment in the laboratory.
- Notify my teacher immediately of an emergency.
- NEVER work alone in the laboratory.
- NEVER eat or drink in the laboratory unless instructed to do so by my teacher.
- Handle living organisms or preserved specimens only when authorized by my teacher, and then, with respect.
- NEVER enter or work in a supply area unless instructed to do so and supervised by my teacher.

[This portion of the contract is to be kept by the student.]

[Return this portion to your teacher.]

I, _____, [print name] have read each of the statements in the Student Science Laboratory Safety Contract and understand these safety rules. I agree to abide by the safety regulations and any additional written or verbal instructions provided by the school district or my teacher. I further agree to follow all other written and verbal instructions given in class.

_____   _____
Student Signature   Date

I acknowledge that my child/ward has signed this contract in good faith.

_____   _____
Parent/Guardian Signature   Date

 **Laboratory Activity**

A Scientific Method

When scientists are asked questions, they might not know the answers. They think of the possible answers, called hypotheses, and experiment to find the correct answers. Using the results of the experiment, they might need to form another hypothesis and test it. This way of solving a problem is called a scientific method.

Strategy

You will predict whether or not red cabbage juice will remain red when chemicals are added to it.
You will test your prediction with an experiment.
You will observe what happens and record your observations.
You will draw conclusions based on your observations.

Materials

graduated cylinder (25 mL)
40 mL red cabbage juice
test-tube rack
4 test tubes (18 × 150-mm)
vinegar (Keep containers closed when not in use.)

ammonia
baking soda solution
labels
3 droppers

CAUTION: *Do not mix ammonia with vinegar. May react vigorously.*
CAUTION: *Ammonia fumes are poisonous. Avoid inhaling the vapors.*
CAUTION: *Do not taste, eat, or drink any materials used in this lab.*
CAUTION: *Inform your teacher if you come in contact with any chemicals.*

Procedure

1. In the space below, predict what will happen to the red cabbage juice when vinegar, ammonia, and baking soda solution are added to it.

   _____

   _____

2. Label four test tubes, 1, 2, 3, and 4.
3. Add 10 mL of red cabbage juice to each test tube.

CAUTION: *Avoid contacting any chemicals with clothes or skin. Rinse with water if spilled.*
4. Add 10 drops of vinegar to test tube 1.
5. Add 10 drops of ammonia to test tube 2.
6. Add 10 drops of baking soda solution to test tube 3.
7. Do not add anything to test tube 4. This is the control. The control is the part of the experiment that is not tested.
8. Record your observations in the Table.

Data and Observations

Test tube	Substance added	Color
1		
2		
3		
4		

Laboratory Activity 1 (continued)

Questions and Conclusions

1. a. Was your prediction correct?

_____

b. What part of the scientific method is predicting?

_____

2. Do all chemicals have the same effect on red cabbage juice?

_____

3. Why did you record the color changes?

_____

_____

_____

4. What steps in the scientific method did you use?

_____

_____

5. What is the purpose of the control in an experiment?

_____

_____

6. Why is a hypothesis called an educated guess?

_____

_____

7. Was your experimenting a way of proving your hypothesis?

_____

_____

8. How did your hypothesis change after experimenting?

_____

_____

Strategy Check

_____ Can you make a prediction?

_____ Can you test your prediction and record what happened?

_____ Can you draw conclusions based on your observations?

Using a Scientific Method

Chapter 1

If scientists hypothesized that there are organisms in the air, how could they test their hypothesis? Do you believe that there are organisms in the air? What makes you think so? You can experiment to test your hypothesis.

Strategy
You will use a scientific method to determine if organisms are found in the air.
You will use tubes containing various foods that may or may not allow for the growth of organisms.
You will observe and test for the presence of organisms.

Materials

4 test tubes (18 × 150-mm)	4 test-tube holders	cotton balls
graduated cylinder	beaker (oven proof, 250-mL)	labels
bouillon soup	hot plate	litmus paper (red or blue)
water	test-tube rack	

Procedure

1. Pour 15 mL of bouillon soup into two test tubes.
2. Add 15 mL of water to two other test tubes.
3. Place each test tube into a test-tube holder and then place all the holders into a small beaker half filled with water. Place the beaker on a hot plate. Allow the tubes to remain in the water for at least 15 min. while boiling.
4. Remove all tubes from the hot water bath. **CAUTION:** *Do not touch the tubes. They are hot.*
5. Place the test tubes in a test-tube rack. Seal one bouillon tube and one water tube securely with a cotton plug. Leave the remaining two tubes open.
6. Label each tube with your name, date, and either "water" or "soup."
7. Examine all the tubes after one week. Compare the appearance of the two tubes containing soup. Are they cloudy or clear? Hold them toward the light to help decide. Record your observations using the words *cloudy* or *clear* under the column marked *Appearance* in Table 1. Compare the appearance of the two water tubes. Again use *cloudy* or *clear* under Appearance in the table.

8. Test each test tube to determine if the liquids are acid, base, or neutral. Remove the cotton plugs and dip a small piece of litmus paper into each tube. Use a new piece of litmus paper for each tube. HINT: Blue litmus turns red in an acid and red litmus turns blue in a base. No change in either paper means that the liquid is neutral. Use the words *acid, base,* or *neutral* to complete the column marked *Litmus paper test* in the table.
9. Carefully smell each tube. See the figure below. Record in the column marked *Odor* in the table whether the tubes smell meaty, spoiled, or have no smell (none).
10. Give all test tubes to your teacher for proper disposal.

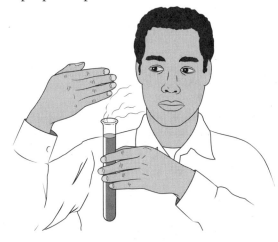

Copyright © Glencoe/McGraw-Hill, a division of the McGraw-Hill Companies, Inc.

Laboratory Activity 2 (continued)

Data and Observations

Table 1

Tube	Appearance	Litmus paper test	Odor
1. soup, open			
2. soup, sealed			
3. water, open			
4. water, sealed			

Questions and Conclusions

1. Bacteria growing in a liquid will cause the liquid to become cloudy. Which tube(s) had bacteria growing in them? Which tube(s) remained clear?

_____

_____

2. Bacteria growing in a liquid cause the liquid to change to an acid. Comparing the litmus paper test between the opened and sealed soup tubes, which tube(s) became acid? Which tube(s) remained neutral?

_____

_____

3. Bacteria growing in a liquid often results in a spoiled odor. Which tube(s) had a spoiled odor?

_____

_____

4. Bacteria will grow in liquids only if a food supply is present. Which tube(s) contained food? Which tube(s) had no food available for bacteria (water is not a food)?

_____

_____

_____

Laboratory Activity 2 (continued)

5. What evidence do you have that bacteria came into the tubes only from the air?

_____

_____

_____

6. What evidence do you have that bacteria need food in order to live, grow, and increase in number?

_____

_____

7. Why were all the tubes first boiled in hot water? **HINT**: Boiling destroys bacteria.

_____

_____

8. What conclusion can you make if the sealed soup tube became cloudy and had a foul odor?

_____

_____

9. What evidence do you have that you breathe organisms as part of the air?

_____

_____

_____

10. Predict what experimental results might be expected if both tubes of soup and water were boiled and sealed. Explain.

_____

_____

11. Predict what experimental results might be expected if both tubes of soup were boiled but were left open.

_____

_____

12. Predict what experimental results might be expected if both tubes were not boiled and were not sealed.

_____

_____

Strategy Check

_____ Did you use a scientific method to test the hypothesis that there are organisms in the air?

_____ Can you determine which tubes do or do not have organisms growing in them?

Getting Close to the Moon

Chapter 2

The last 50 years have been one of the most exciting times in history for humans and space exploration. In 1969, the first person landed on the Moon and returned safely to Earth. On that trip and several subsequent trips to the Moon, astronauts brought back rocks and took pictures of places that had only been seen before with telescopes. In this lab you will examine a picture of the surface of the Moon and collect your own data about some features of the lunar landscape.

Strategy

You will learn some of the features of the Moon's surface.
You will collect data about some lunar features.
You will make inferences about how some of these features developed.

Materials

red pencil
ruler (in centimeters)

Procedure

1. Examine the picture of the Moon in Figure 1 of this exercise.
2. Find the craters named Kepler, Copernicus, Hercules, Atlas, and Plato. Circle each with your pencil.
3. Locate and circle the maria, or seas, which are large, dry depressions on the Moon's surface, called Mare Serenitatus, Mare Tranquillitatus, and Mare Nectaris.
4. There are also mountains on the Moon. Find the Caucasus Mountains and circle them.
5. Using your ruler, measure the distance from the center of Mare Nectaris to the edge of the crater Theophilus. Repeat this measurement to the edge of Mare Fecunditatis. Draw a triangle that connects the center of the two maria and the crater edge. Record your data in Table 1 in the Data and Observations section.

6. Remember that you read that craters are caused by meteorites. Find crater Copernicus and notice a wide spray of dust lying around the crater. This kind of debris is called "ejecta." Measure the diameter of the ejecta spray from north to south. Record this in your table. Then measure the diameter of the ejecta spray from east to west. Record this also.

Laboratory Activity 1 (continued)

Figure 1

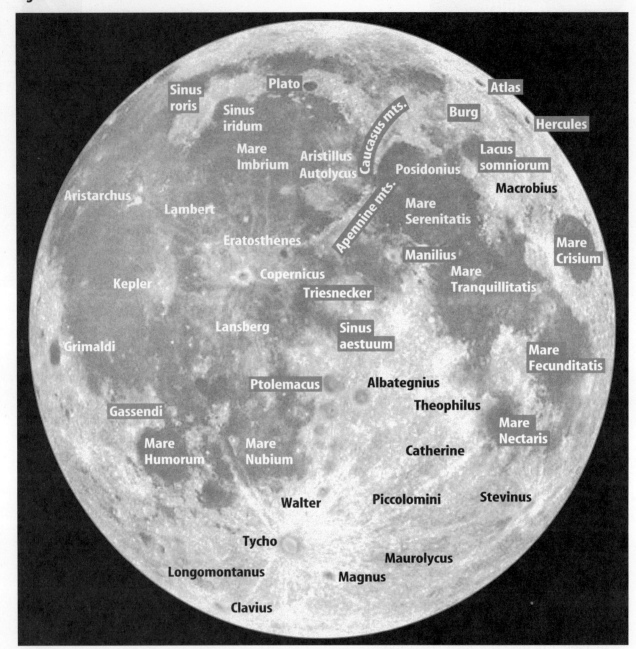

Laboratory Activity 1 (continued)

Data and Observations

Table 1

Moon Surface	Distance in centimeters
Center of Mare Nectaris to Crater Theophilus	1.
Center of Mare Nectaris to Mare Fecunditatus	2.
Mare Fecunditatus to Crater Theophilus	3.
Total distance between Mare Fecunditatus, Crater Theophilus, and Mare Nectaris	4. 1+2+3=
Copernicus ejecta field from north to south	5.
Copernicus ejecta field from east to west	6.

Questions and Conclusions

1. Why do you think the Copernicus ejecta field is longer than it is wide?

_____

_____

_____

_____

_____

2. None of the rock samples the astronauts brought back contains fossils. What conclusion can you draw from this fact?

_____

_____

_____

_____

_____

Laboratory Activity 1 (continued)

3. There are no complete maps of the far side of the Moon. Why do you think this is so?

_____

_____

4. Some of the craters, like Kepler and Copernicus, are named for famous astronomers. There are so many craters on the Moon that not all of them have been named. Pick a crater and draw a star around it. If you could name the crater anything you like, what would it be? Write that name on your map near the crater and on the line below. Explain why you chose that name.

_____

_____

Strategy Check

_____ Can you locate some of the features of the Moon's surface?

_____ Can you collect data about some lunar features?

_____ Can you infer how some lunar features developed?

Building a Sundial

For centuries, people have used the shadows cast by the Sun to measure time. As Earth turns, the Sun appears to move across the sky, and shadows change as the position of the Sun changes. The rotation of Earth is very steady and constant. This makes the changing shadows a good way to measure the length of time in a day. People in ancient times used a small stick to make a shadow on the ground. They used the changes in the position of the stick's shadow in relation to the stick itself to tell time.

Today, most people think that sundials are not very accurate and that a watch is better for telling time. This is not true. Sundials are very precise as long as they are correctly placed. People who know a lot about sundials are very good at putting them in the right place and at the correct angle. It takes a lot of practice. In this lab you will make a simple sundial and show how the shadow of the Sun moves across your dial.

Strategy
You will build a model of a horizontal type of sundial.
You will determine how to place your sundial to show that sundials keep accurate time.

Materials
stiff card paper or construction paper
ruler (cm)
protractor
compass

scissors
drinking straw
atlas

Procedure
1. Cut your paper into a strip 30 cm long and 20 cm wide.
2. Draw a line across your paper 2 cm from the top and another line 15 cm from the top. Draw a third line across the paper 1 cm from the bottom. Label the lines A, B, and C. See Figure 1 on the next page.
3. Use your ruler to mark a point in the center of line A. This will be your reference point for the center of your protractor and will also be the point where you will place one end of your straw.
4. On both sides of your paper, draw a semicircle around the edge of the protractor using the center mark as your reference point. Make marks at 15 degree intervals on each of the two semicircles. Number the hours as shown in Figure 1.
5. Fold the paper along line B. See Figure 1. Make a small tab by cutting and bending a piece of your paper in the middle of line C. This should fit into one end of your straw. Now make a hole in the center of line A and insert the other end of your straw.

6. Use an atlas to find the latitude of your school. Use this number to make an arc of the same degree between the straw and the horizontal part of the paper lying on your table. The straw now represents the part of a sundial called the gnomon. The shadow of the gnomon will fall on the top side of your dial in the summer and the underside in the winter.
7. Now, take your sundial and a compass outdoors and find the direction north. Place your sundial in a direct line with north and mark the spot the shadow hits. Check your sundial every 10 or 15 min and note in the Data and Observations table any changes that occur in the position of the shadow.

Laboratory Activity 2 (continued)

Figure 1

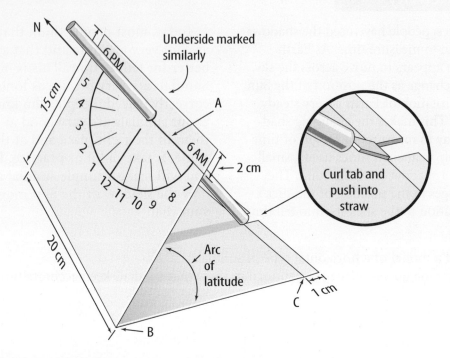

Data and Observations

Time shown by shadow on sundial	Angles in degrees

Questions and Conclusions

1. Why does the shadow on the sundial move with time?

_____

_____

_____

2. It is always important to adjust your sundial for the latitude in which you live. Why?

_____

_____

_____

Laboratory Activity 2 (continued)

3. It is obvious that a sundial would not work at night. Under what other conditions would it be impractical to use a sundial?

_____

_____

_____

4. There are two places on Earth that, at certain times of the year, a sundial will work continuously. Where are these two places and when would they work without stopping?

_____

_____

_____

Strategy Check

_____ Can you build a model of a horizontal type of sundial?

_____ Can you determine how to place your sundial to show that it keeps accurate time?

Mixtures and Compounds

Chapter 3

Matter is anything that has mass and occupies space. Matter exists in different forms. Three classifications of matter are well known to us: elements, mixtures, and compounds. Elements are the basic materials of our world. Elements in a mixture have recognizable boundaries and can be separated by mechanical means. Elements that form a chemical compound can be separated only by a chemical process. The element oxygen(O) combines with the element hydrogen (H) to form water (H_2O), which is a compound. Salt water is a mixture of two compounds, water and salt.

Strategy

You will separate a mixture into its parts.
You will compare the characteristics of a compound and a mixture.

Materials

magnifying glass   water
sand (coarse)   disposable pie pans (2)
granite rock   rock salt
granite (crushed)   heat source

Procedure

1. Use the magnifying glass to observe the sand and granite rock. Sketch the granite with the minerals in it, and the shapes of the sand grains under Sketch A.
2. Sort the crushed granite into separate piles according to color.
3. Sketch the general shape of a piece from each pile of the sorted granite, and label each as to color under Sketch B.
4. Mix a spoonful of sand in some water in a pie pan. Sketch what you observed under Sketch C.

5. Examine and sketch the salt crystals under Sketch D. **CAUTION:** *Do not ingest rock salt. It might contain harmful impurities.*
6. Mix a spoonful of salt in some water in the second pie pan. Record your observations.
7. Heat both pans until the water is evaporated. Sketch what is left in each pan under Sketch E. **CAUTION:** *Be careful not to get clothes or hair close to the heat source.*

Data and Observations

Sketch A

Sketch B

Laboratory Activity 1 (continued)

Sketch C

Sketch D

Sketch E

Questions and Conclusions

1. Are any of the sand grains similar to any of the granite fragments? If so, describe them.

_____

_____

2. How are salt and sand similar? How are they different?

_____

_____

3. Is salt water a compound or a mixture? Explain.

_____

_____

4. Is granite a compound or a mixture? Explain.

_____

_____

5. Name some mechanical processes used to separate mixtures.

_____

_____

Strategy Check

_____ Can you separate components of a mixture?

_____ Can you tell the difference between a compound and a mixture?

LAB 2 Laboratory Activity

Constructing Compounds

All elements are made of atoms. Compounds are formed when two or more elements combine to form a different type of matter. A chemical formula is a shortcut chemists take to describe a specific compound. It tells the numbers and types of atoms that make up a single unit of a compound. You probably already know that the formula for one common compound—water—is H_2O. The formula for water tells us that a molecule of water has two hydrogen atoms and one oxygen atom.

Strategy

You will build models of different compounds.

You will use your models to determine how many atoms of each element are in each molecule.

Materials

modeling clay (red, yellow, and blue)
toothpicks

Procedure

1. Obtain enough clay to make four balls of each color. Each clay ball represents one atom of an element. Blue balls represent hydrogen atoms, red balls represent oxygen atoms, and yellow balls represent carbon atoms.

2. Using toothpicks to connect your clay atoms as shown Figure 1, construct a model of each of the following compounds. After you construct each model, fill in the blanks for that compound in the table in the Data and Observations section. After you finish making the molecules for water and carbon dioxide, take them apart. Then make the methane molecule.

   a. H_2O (water): Connect two hydrogen atoms to one oxygen atom.

   b. CO_2 (carbon dioxide): Connect two oxygen atoms to one carbon atom.

   c. CH_4 (methane): Connect four hydrogen atoms to one carbon atom.

Figure 1

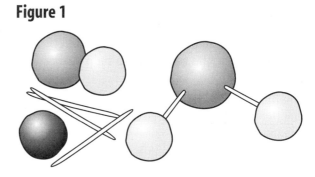

Laboratory Activity 2 (continued)

Data and Observations

Chemical formula	Number of atoms in compound			
	Hydrogen	Carbon	Oxygen	Total
1. H_2O (water)				
2. CO_2 (carbon dioxide)				
3. CH_4 (methane)				

Questions and Conclusions

1. What would the answers in the table be for a molecule of fruit sugar, $C_6H_{12}O_6$?

_____

2. From the formulas given, identify each of the following as either an element or a compound: NaCl, Ag, Co, CO, SO_2, AgBr.

_____

_____

3. Each carbon atom can be attached to up to four other atoms. The compound hexane has six carbon atoms joined together in a chain. If only carbon and hydrogen make up the hexane molecule, what is the greatest number of hydrogen atoms that could be in the molecule? Draw a picture of the molecule to help you.

_____

_____

4. Nitrogen in air is in the form of two nitrogen atoms fastened together, N_2. Is nitrogen an element or is it a compound? Explain.

_____

_____

Strategy Check

_____ Can you make a simple model of a compound based on its molecular formula?

_____ Based on a compound's molecular formula, can you figure out how many atoms of each element are in a compound?

_____ Do you understand the difference between an element and a compound?

Comparing Viscosity

You have probably noticed that pushing a spoon with a small force moves it easily through a bowl of water. However, the same force moves a spoon through a thick milkshake much more slowly. Viscosity is a physical property of a fluid (liquids and gases) that tends to prevent it from flowing when it is subjected to an applied force. There are many ways to measure viscosity. One way is seeing how fast a fluid pours through a hole. The faster a fluid flows, the lower the viscosity of the fluid. Another way to measure viscosity is to see how fast a sphere falls through a fluid. If a fluid has a high viscosity, it strongly resists flow, so the sphere falls slowly. If the fluid has a low viscosity, it offers less resistance to flow, so the sphere falls faster. In this activity, you will use both methods to compare the viscosities of several liquids.

Strategy

You will construct a viscometer to determine the flow time for a specific volume of water.

You will use a viscometer to determine the flow times for other liquids.

You will rank the relative viscosities of the other liquids by comparing their flow times with that of water.

You will compare the viscosities of liquids by dropping glass marbles into samples of liquids.

You will observe how temperature affects the viscosity of a liquid.

Materials

clear-plastic dish detergent bottle with pull top, bottom removed
marking pen
ruler
modeling clay
glass jar
room temperature water
timer, or clock with second hand
vegetable oil
dishwashing liquid
corn syrup or molasses
4 50-mL graduated cylinders
4 glass marbles
long-handled spoon
2 25-mL graduated cylinders
2 large beakers
hot tap water
ice water
thermometer
paper towels

Procedure

Part A

1. Holding the detergent bottle upside down, use the marking pen to draw a straight line 2.5 cm from the bottom. Draw a second line 10 cm below the first line.

2. Label the first line *Start* and label the second line *Stop.*

3. Close the pull top on the bottle.

4. Place a ring of modeling clay around the top edge of the mouth of a jar.

Figure 1

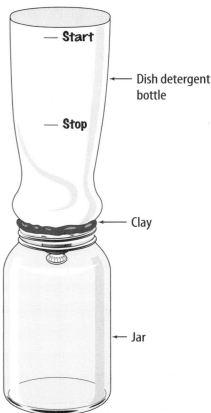

— Start

← Dish detergent bottle

— Stop

← Clay

← Jar

Laboratory Activity 1 (continued)

5. Stand the bottle upside down in the jar and mold the clay ring so that the bottle will stand upright without falling over. Do NOT push the bottle into the clay because you will need to be able to easily remove and replace the bottle. Your setup should look like Figure 1.

6. Fill the bottle to about 1 cm above the start line with room temperature tap water.

7. Lift the bottle and pull the top open. Immediately set the bottle back on the jar.

8. Start the timer when the water level reaches the *Start* line. Stop the timer when the water level reaches the *Stop* line. Record the time in Table 1.

9. Repeat steps 6 through 8 two more times. Calculate the average flow rate of the water and record the times in Table 1.

10. Repeat steps 6–8 for the oil, dishwashing liquid, and syrup, remembering to thoroughly clean your viscometer components between each type of liquid. Record your observations in Table 1.

Part B

11. Pour 50 mL of water into one graduated cylinder. Pour 50 mL of oil into second, 50 mL of dishwashing liquid into a third, and 50 mL of syrup into a fourth graduated cylinder.

12. Put two of the graduated cylinders side by side and place them against a white background so you can clearly see what happens.

Figure 2

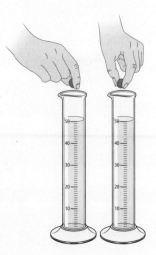

13. Hold a marble in each hand at the same distance above each of the graduated cylinders, as shown in Figure 2.

14. Release both marbles at exactly the same time and observe which reaches the bottom of the graduated cylinder first. Record your observations in Table 2.

15. Use a long-handled spoon to remove the marbles from the graduated cylinders.

16. Repeat steps 14 and 15, changing one liquid each time, until you can put the liquids in order of increasing viscosity.

Part C

17. Pour 25 mL of syrup into each of two 25-mL graduated cylinders.

18. Place one graduated cylinder in a large beaker of hot tap water. Place the other graduated cylinder in second beaker full of ice water.

19. Allow both graduated cylinders to sit for 15 minutes.

20. After 15 minutes, measure the temperature of both samples of syrup. Record the temperatures in Table 3.

21. Remove the graduated cylinders from the beakers.

22. Hold a marble in each hand at the same distance above each of the graduated cylinders.

23. Release both marbles at exactly the same time and observe which reaches the bottom of the graduated cylinder first. Record your observations in Table 3.

Laboratory Activity 1 (continued)

Data and Observations

Table 1

Liquid	Trial 1 time (s)	Trial 2 time (s)	Trial 3 time (s)	Average time (s)
Water				
Oil				
Dishwashing liquid				
Syrup				

Table 2

Liquids	Liquids in which marble reached the bottom of the jar first
Water and oil	Water
Water and dishwashing liquid	Water
Water and syrup	Water
Oil and dishwashing liquid	Oil
Oil and syrup	Oil
Dishwashing liquid and syrup	Dishwashing liquid

Table 3

	Temperature (°C)	Rate of marble drop
Hot syrup		
Cold syrup		

Laboratory Activity 1 (continued)

Questions and Conclusions

1. Based on your data from Part A, rank the four liquids from lowest to highest viscosity.

_____

2. Based on your data from Part B, rank the four liquids from lowest to highest viscosity.

_____

_____

3. Do your rankings in Part B agree with your rankings in Part A? If not, suggest a reason for the differences.

_____

4. How does temperature affect the viscosity of syrup?

_____

_____

_____

5. If the flow time of a sample of shampoo is 580 s and the flow time of an equal volume of water is 40 s, what does this tell you about viscosity of the shampoo relative to water?

_____

_____

Strategy Check

_____ Can you construct a viscometer to determine the flow time for a specific volume of water?

_____ Can you use a viscometer to determine the flow times for other liquids?

_____ Can you rank the relative viscosities of the other liquids by comparing their flow times with that of water?

_____ Can you compare the viscosities of liquids by dropping glass marbles into samples of liquids?

_____ Can you observe how temperature affects the viscosity of a liquid?

Chemical Changes

Chapter 4

When a chemical change takes place, something new is produced. Chemical changes can happen in living matter. Energy is often given off during a chemical change. Energy that is given off may be in different forms, but one form that is easily measured is heat.

Strategy

You will observe chemical changes produced by living matter.
You will measure and record changes in temperature when these chemical changes take place.

Materials

hydrogen peroxide (3%)
18 × 150 mm test tubes (8)
thermometer
liver (raw)

test-tube rack
clock or watch with second hand
potato (raw)

Procedure

Part A

1. Add 5 mL of hydrogen peroxide to a test tube.
   CAUTION: *Hydrogen peroxide is poisonous.*
2. Place a thermometer into the test tube. Find the temperature of the hydrogen peroxide and record this as the temperature before adding the liver. Record all of your results in Table 1 in the Data and Observations section.
3. Remove the thermometer from the test tube.
4. Add a small piece of liver to the test tube.
5. Replace the thermometer and begin to record the temperature of the liver and hydrogen peroxide every half minute for 6 min. See Figure 1.
6. Repeat the experiment three more times. Use new hydrogen peroxide, a new piece of liver, and a clean test tube for each trial.

Part B

1. Add 5 mL of hydrogen peroxide to a test tube.
2. Find the temperature of the hydrogen peroxide. Record your results in Table 2 in the Data and Observations section.
3. Add a small piece of potato to the test tube.
4. Replace the thermometer and record the temperature of the potato and the hydrogen peroxide every half minute for 6 min.

5. Repeat the procedure three more times. Use new hydrogen peroxide, a new piece of potato, and a clean test tube for each trial.

Figure 1

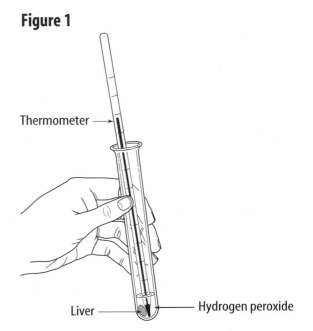

Thermometer →

Liver ——   —— Hydrogen peroxide

Laboratory Activity 2 (continued)

Data and Observations

1. Record your results in the tables.
2. For each table, total each column and find the average for each column.

Table 1

Trial	Starting temperature	Temperature after adding liver											
		Minutes											
		1/2	1	1 1/2	2	2 1/2	3	3 1/2	4	4 1/2	5	5 1/2	6
1													
2													
3													
4													
Total													
Average													

Table 2

Trial	Starting temperature	Temperature after adding potato											
		Minutes											
		1/2	1	1 1/2	2	2 1/2	3	3 1/2	4	4 1/2	5	5 1/2	6
1													
2													
3													
4													
Total													
Average													

Laboratory Activity 2 (continued)

3. Graph your average results for each table. Place a dot on the graph in Figure 2 for the average starting temperature and for each average temperature 1/2 min through 6 min. Connect the dots with lines. Use different colors for each line.

Figure 2

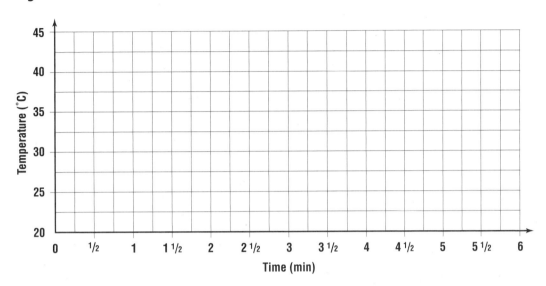

Questions and Conclusions

1. Is there any evidence that energy was given off when liver was added to the hydrogen peroxide?

   _____

2. What is the evidence?

   _____

   _____

   _____

3. Is there any evidence that energy was given off when the potato was added to the hydrogen peroxide?

   _____

4. What is the evidence?

   _____

   _____

   _____

5. How does the evidence indicate that a physical or chemical change has taken place?

   _____

   _____

Laboratory Activity 2 (continued)

6. Why were four trials used for each part of the experiment?

_____

_____

7. Why were both liver and potato used in the experiment?

_____

_____

8. Which showed the greatest temperature change, potato or liver?

_____

9. During the experiment, hydrogen peroxide was changed into water and oxygen. Did you see anything during the experiment that shows that oxygen was given off?

_____

_____

10. Explain your answer.

_____

_____

_____

Strategy Check

_____ Can you observe chemical changes produced by living matter?

_____ Can you measure and record changes in temperature when chemical changes take place?

Speed of Falling Objects

Galileo attempted to prove that objects of different mass will reach the ground at the same time when dropped from the same height. But this was difficult, since the objects fell so quickly he couldn't tell whether or not they actually hit the ground together. Galileo thought that if he could slow down the objects, he would be able to make more accurate observations.

Strategy

You will show the speeds of falling objects of different mass.

You will compare the speeds of falling objects of different mass.

Materials

masking tape
15 cm × 150 cm gutter
*15 cm × 150 cm board with sides
chair
2 marbles (each of different mass)
index card
*Alternate Materials

Procedure

1. Place a strip of masking tape straight across each end of the gutter (one near each end of the board). See Figure 1.

2. Rest one end of the gutter on top of the back of the chair. (The top of the gutter should be at shoulder height or higher.) See Figure 1.

3. Place both marbles on one edge of the tape at the top of the gutter. This is the starting line.

4. Have your partner position himself or herself near the tape at the bottom. This is the finish line.

5. Hold an index card in front of the marbles. Raise it to release both marbles at the same time.

6. Have your partner watch to see the order in which the marbles cross the finish line.

7. Record the results by putting a checkmark in the appropriate column in Table 1 in the Data and Observations section.

8. Repeat the experiment two more times with the marbles positioned as in step 3.

9. Exchange the position of the marbles at the starting line and run the experiment three more times (six times in all). Record your results.

10. Repeat the experiment placing the gutter at a different angle to the floor. Record your results in Table 2.

Figure 1

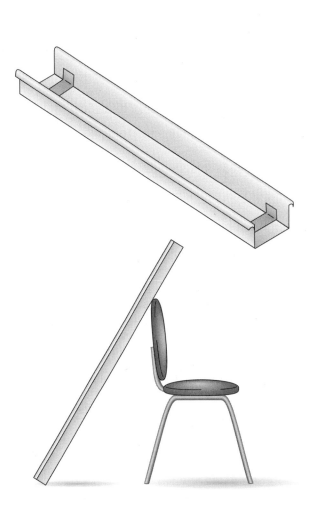

Laboratory Activity 1 (continued)

Data and Observations

Table 1

Slope _____			
Trial	Large marble went faster	Small marble went faster	Both went at same speed
1			
2			
3			
4			
5			
6			

Table 2

Slope _____			
Trial	Large marble went faster	Small marble went faster	Both went at same speed
1			
2			
3			
4			
5			
6			

Questions and Conclusions

1. How do the speeds of the rolling marbles compare?

_____

_____

2. Was there any difference in speed after you exchanged positions of the marbles?

_____

_____

Laboratory Activity 1 (continued)

3. Why might it be important to change the position of the marbles for one half of the trials?

_____

_____

4. Compare and contrast your results with the ramp at different angles.

_____

_____

_____

5. What can you conclude about the speed of falling objects of different mass?

_____

_____

_____

6. Compare and contrast the motion of marbles rolling down the ramp with the motion of marbles that are dropped.

_____

_____

_____

_____

Strategy Check

_____ Can you show the speeds of falling objects of different mass?

_____ Can you compare the speeds of falling objects of different mass?

Newton's First Law of Motion

Chapter 5

One of Isaac Newton's laws of motion states that all bodies at rest tend to remain at rest unless a force acts on them. However, once a body is set in motion by an outside force, the body moves in a straight line until another force causes it to change speed or direction. The force that changes the motion of the body may be air pressure, friction, or another body.

Strategy

You will measure the amount of force needed to set a body in motion.

You will deduce the relationship between the force needed to start a body in motion and the mass of the body.

Materials

balance
bricks
spring scale

Procedure

1. Determine the mass of one brick. Record it in Table 1.
2. Attach the brick to the spring scale. Pull the brick slowly across the floor.
3. Record the force needed to start the brick in motion. Record the force needed to keep the brick in motion.
4. Determine the mass of the second brick. Add that to the mass of the first brick and record it in Table 1.

5. Repeat steps 2 and 3 with the second brick on top of the first brick.
6. Determine the mass of the third brick. Add that to the mass of the other bricks and record it in Table 1.
7. Repeat steps 2 and 3 with the third brick on top of the other two bricks.

Data and Observations

Table 1

Number of bricks	Mass (kg)	Force (N)	
		Start	Keep in motion
1			
2			
3			

Laboratory Activity 2 (continued)

Questions and Conclusions

1. What is the outside force that starts the brick(s) in motion?

   _____

2. Compare the force needed to start the brick(s) in motion and the force needed to keep the brick(s) in motion.

   _____

   _____

   _____

3. Compare the force required to keep the brick(s) in motion to the mass of the brick(s).

   _____

   _____

   _____

4. State the relationship between the force needed to start a body in motion and the body's mass.

   _____

   _____

   _____

5. What force resists the motion of the bricks in all cases?

   _____

6. Explain in terms of Newton's law of motion what happens to a passenger who is standing in the aisle of a bus when the bus stops suddenly. Use diagrams to help explain your answer.

   _____

   _____

   _____

Strategy Check

_____ Can you measure the amount of force needed to set a body in motion?

_____ Can you state the relationship between the force needed to start a body in motion and the mass of the body?

Radiation

Have you ever walked barefoot on asphalt on a sunny summer day? The black pavement is hot because it absorbs energy transferred from the Sun by radiation. Radiation is the movement of energy in the form of waves. Different materials absorb radiant energy from the sun differently. In today's experiment, you will compare how light-colored materials and dark-colored materials differ in their ability to absorb energy from the sun.

Strategy

You will observe how energy from the Sun can increase the temperature of water.
You will determine how color influences how much solar radiation is absorbed.

Materials

construction paper (black)
construction paper (white)
containers (2 plastic, 500-mL)
scissors
tape
graduated cylinder (100-mL)
water
thermometer (alcohol, Celsius)
timer
pencils (colored)

Procedure

CAUTION: *Use care when handling sharp objects.*
1. Fasten black construction paper on the bottom and sides of one container.
2. Fasten white construction paper on the bottom and sides of the other container.
3. Add 250 mL of room-temperature water to each container.
4. Use a thermometer to find the temperature of the water in each container. Record your data in Table 1 in the Data and Observations section.
5. Place the containers side by side in direct sunlight outside on a sunny windowsill. Be sure both containers receive the same amount of sunshine.
6. Measure the temperature of the water in each container at 5-minute intervals for 30 minutes. Record your data in Table 1.
7. Using Figure 2, graph the data from the table, using a line graph. Use one colored pencil to show data for the light container and a different one to show data for the dark container. Draw lines to connect the temperature for each container of water.

Figure 1

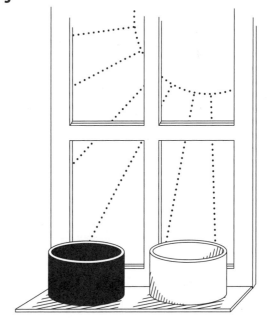

Copyright © Glencoe/McGraw-Hill, a division of the McGraw-Hill Companies, Inc.

Laboratory Activity 1 (continued)

Data and Observations

Table 1

Color of container	Time (min)						
	0	5	10	15	20	25	30
Temp. (°C)—Light							
Temp. (°C)—Dark							

Figure 2

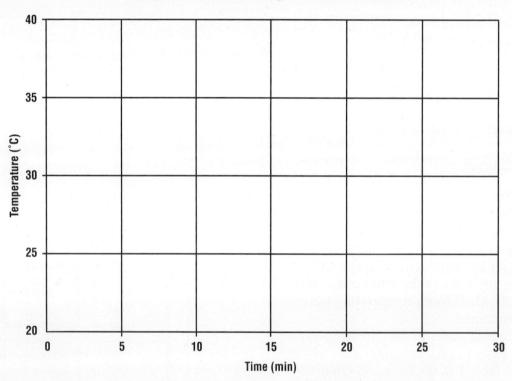

Temperature of Water in Light and Dark Containers

1. What was the final temperature of the water in the dark container?

   _____

2. What was the final temperature of the water in the light container?

   _____

3. How many degrees did the temperature of the water in the dark container increase?

   _____

4. How many degrees did the temperature of the water in the light container increase?

   _____

Laboratory Activity 1 (continued)

Questions and Conclusions

1. Did one container of water heat up more quickly? Which one?

   _____

2. How do you think the color of an object affects how it absorbs energy from the Sun?

   _____

   _____

   _____

3. Would you get similar results if you placed the containers in the shade? Why or why not?

   _____

   _____

4. If you were stranded in a hot desert, would you rather be wearing a dark-colored or a light-colored T-shirt? Why?

   _____

   _____

   _____

Strategy Check

_____ Can you observe the influence of solar radiation on water temperature?

_____ Can you determine how color influences the absorption of solar radiation?

Chemical Potential Energy— You Are What You Eat!

LAB 2 Laboratory Activity

Chapter 6

What did you eat for breakfast this morning? The food you ate this morning contains chemical energy that your body needs. Energy in the chemical bonds in food supplies the fuel your body needs to keep its temperature steady, help your organs function, and move your muscles. How is energy from food measured? The calorie is the unit scientists use to measure the amount of energy contained in foods. High-calorie foods contain a lot of energy. In this activity, you will compare the energy content of different breakfast cereals and calculate how much time exercising the energy will support.

Strategy

You will compare the energy content of different packaged breakfast cereals by looking at their calorie content.

You will calculate how many hours of activity one serving of cereal provides.

Materials

food labels from various breakfast cereals (4)

Procedure

Figure 1

Nutrition Facts

Serving Size   About 3/4 cup
Servings per container   About 11

Amount Per Serving	Cereal	Cereal with 1/2 cup Vitamin A & D Skim Milk
Calories Per Serving	180	220
Calories from Fat	10	10
	% Daily Value **	
Total Fat 1.0g*	2%	2%
Saturated Fat 0g	0%	0%
Monounsaturated Fat 0g		
Polyunsaturated Fat 0.5g		

1. Look at the Nutrition Facts label on four different breakfast cereals (Figure 1). The number of calories contained in one serving of cereal is listed at the top of the Nutrition Facts label. In Table 1 in the Data and Observations section, record the name of each cereal and the number of calories in one serving with milk.

2. Table 2 lists the number of calories needed to perform different activities for 1 h. From Table 1, select one of the cereals you examined and calculate the number of hours of each activity it would take to use the calories in one serving of cereal. Use the following equation.

$$\text{Hours of activity provided by 1 serving of cereal} = \frac{\text{calories in 1 serving of cereal}}{\text{calories needed for 1 hour of activity}}$$

Laboratory Activity 2 (continued)

Data and Observations

Table 1

Name of cereal	Number of calories per serving (with milk)

Name of cereal from Table 1 chosen to use in Table 2

_____

Table 2

Type of activity	Calories used per hour	Number of hours required to use the energy in 1 serving of cereal
Sleeping	56	
Standing	112	
Walking	210	
Running	850	

Questions and Conclusions

1. Based on the number of calories in each breakfast cereal, which cereal provides the most energy per serving?

   _____

2. Why is the calorie content different for cereal with milk and for cereal without milk?

   _____

3. Why do you feel warmer when you exercise?

   _____

4. Is the energy in food potential energy or kinetic energy?

Strategy Check

_____ Can you compare the energy content of different breakfast cereals?

_____ Can you calculate how many hours of activity are required to use the energy in one serving of a specific breakfast cereal?

Shapes of Bacteria

Thousands of different types of bacteria are known and have been observed, and there are possibly many more that have not yet been observed. How can a scientist tell those organisms apart when they are so small? One way is by their characteristic shapes, or patterns of joining together in groups.

Strategy

You will identify bacteria by using their shape and other characteristics as clues.
You will discover a process of elimination or "key" that will be used to help in the identification.

Materials

key on next page

Procedure

1. Examine Figure 1 in Data and Observations, which shows bacteria magnified 2,000 times their natural size.
2. Use the key on the next page to identify each type of bacterium. Start at the top of the key, following the directions. The key will allow you to identify each bacterium by name. Each bacterium has a first name that describes its shape in scientific language, and a last name that may also describe some special characteristic. The key also lists in parentheses the disease caused by the bacterium or type of food in which the bacterium may be found. Label each bacterium in Data and Observations.

Data and Observations

Figure 1

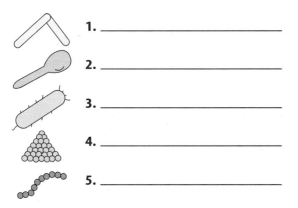

1. _____

2. _____

3. _____

4. _____

5. _____

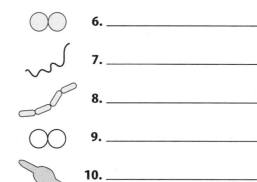

6. _____

7. _____

8. _____

9. _____

10. _____

Laboratory Activity 1 (continued)

Key
If the general shape of a bacterium is round, go to I, skip II and III.
If the general shape of a bacterium is rod (long and straight), go to II, skip I and III.
If the general shape of a bacterium is spiral, go to III, skip II and I.

Section I
If in pairs, go to *a* or *a´* only.
If in chains, go to *b* only.
If in clumps, go to *c* only.
a—without a heavy cover—*Diplococcus meningitidis* (causes spinal meningitis)
a´—with a heavy cover (capsule)—*Diplococcus pneumoniae* (causes pneumonia)
b—small in size—*Streptococcus lactis* (found in buttermilk)
c—*Staphylococcus aureus* (causes boils)

Section II
If in chains, go to d only.
If in pairs, go to e only.
If single, go to f or f´ or f˝.
d—*Bacillus anthracis* (causes anthrax)
e—*Bacillus lactis* (found in sauerkraut)
f—with hairs (flagella)—*Bacillus typhosa* (causes typhoid fever)
f˝—with a bulge (spore) in the middle—
Bacillus botulinum (causes botulism poisoning)
f˝—with a bulge at the end—*Bacillus tetani* (causes tetanus)

Section III
Treponema palladium (causes syphilis)

Questions and Conclusions

1. What part of the word is the same for all bacteria found in Section I? _____ ;

   This word refers to the shape of a bacterium. The shape is _____.

2. The word "diplo-" when placed in front of a bacterium name must mean _____.

3. The word "strepto-" when placed in front of a bacterium name must mean _____.

4. The word "staphylo-" when placed in front of a bacterium name must mean _____.

5. What word is the same for all bacteria found in Section II? _____ ;

   This word refers to the shape of a bacterium. The shape is _____.

6. Some bacteria produce chemicals that provide food with a certain taste. Name two such foods.

   _____

Strategy Check

_____ Can you use the key to identify bacteria by their shape and other characteristics?

_____ Can you understand how the use of scientific names helps to describe certain features of bacteria?

LAB 2 Laboratory Activity

Molds

Chapter 7

Molds are fungi that need food for energy. They contain no chlorophyll, so they cannot make their own food. Will molds grow on almost any surface that provides them with food? Will they grow only on surfaces that provide certain conditions?

Strategy

You will build an apparatus to test for mold growth.

You will test the conditions in which mold will grow by using different foods, different light conditions, and different amounts of moisture.

You will observe and record the conditions in which molds grow.

Materials

8 baby food jars (with lids)
potato flakes (dried)
spoon
paper towels
mold source
cotton swab
graduated cylinder (10-mL)
water
labels
pen or pencil

Procedure

1. Your teacher will assign a group with which you will work. Your group will prepare eight jars for testing mold growth.

2. Put a spoonful of dry potato flakes in each of four baby food jars. Put a crumpled paper towel in each of the other four jars.

3. Observe and record in Data and Observations the appearance of mold your teacher supplies to you.
   CAUTION: *Give all swabs to your teacher for proper disposal. Do not touch face or mouth. Always wash your hands after handling microbes.*

4. Rub a cotton swab on the surface of the mold and then rub it on the surface of the towels in the four jars. Rub the swab on the surface of the mold again. Then rub it on the surface of the potato flakes in the other four jars.

5. Put 5 mL of water into each of two potato jars and two paper towel jars.

6. Seal all of the jars with lids. Label the jars with your name and the date. Also write the growth conditions for the four potato and four paper towel jars on each label: dry-dark, dry-light, wet-dark, wet-light.

7. Place the potato jar labeled dry-light in the light and the potato jar labeled dry-dark in the dark. Your teacher will tell you the best places to put your jars. Place the potato jar labeled wet-light in the light and the one labeled wet-dark in the dark. Do the same for the wet and dry paper towel jars.

8. Observe the jars every day for one school week. Record your daily observations in Table 1 under Data and Observations.
   CAUTION: *Give all jars to your teacher for proper disposal.*

Laboratory Activity 2 (continued)

Data and Observations
Appearance of mold:

_____

Table 1

Conditions	Day 1	Day 2	Day 3	Day 4	Day 5
1. Potato-dry-light					
2. Potato-dry-dark					
3. Potato-wet-light					
4. Potato-wet-dark					
5. Towel-dry-light					
6. Towel-dry-dark					
7. Towel-wet-light					
8. Towel-wet-dark					

Appearance of mold growing in any jar after several days:

_____

Questions and Conclusions

1. Is the new mold growing in the jar similar to the original mold? Give evidence of this.

_____

_____

2. Does mold require food in order to grow? Give evidence of this.

_____

3. Does mold require water to grow if food is supplied? Give evidence of this.

_____

4. Does mold grow better in light or dark conditions if food and moisture are supplied? Give

evidence of this. _____

_____

Strategy Check

_____ Can you build an apparatus for testing mold growth?

_____ Can you test mold growth in different conditions?

_____ Can you determine from your results if mold needs food and/or water to grow?

Earthworm Anatomy

Chapter 8

The earthworm is an invertebrate that has a segmented body and specialized body parts. Oxygen from the air moves into its body through its moist skin. Carbon dioxide moves out of its body through the skin. The earthworm has a closed circulatory system with five heart-like structures, called aortic arches. All the worm's blood is contained in blood vessels. The segmented body plan makes an earthworm's anatomy easy to study.

Strategy
You will observe the external parts of an earthworm.
You will dissect an earthworm.
You will identify the internal organs and organ systems of an earthworm.

Materials
dissecting pan with wax
earthworm (preserved)
hand lens
dissecting pins
dissecting scissors
dissecting needle

Procedure

Part A—External Structure
1. Place a preserved earthworm lengthwise in the dissecting pan with the darker side up. This is the dorsal or top side. **CAUTION:** *Wash hands thoroughly after handling worm.*
2. Examine the external structure and identify the parts shown in Figure 1.
3. Run your fingers lightly across the top, bottom, and both sides of the earthworm. The bristles that you feel are called setae.

Examine the setae with a hand lens. Estimate the number of setae on each segment.
4. Locate the mouth. The part that hangs over the mouth is called the prostonium.
5. Find the thickened band circling the body. This is the clitellum. It forms a cocoon for depositing the eggs during reproduction.
6. Locate the anus (see Figure 1).

Figure 1

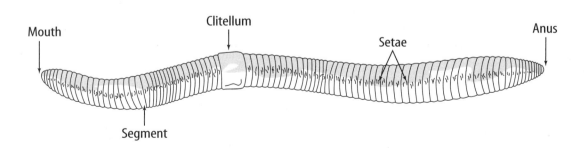

Mouth   Clitellum   Setae   Anus

Segment

Laboratory Activity 1 (continued)

Figure 2

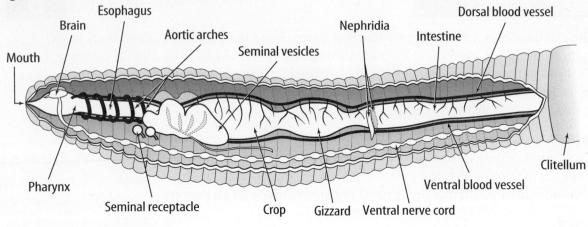

Part B—Internal Structure

Directions: *Read the instructions carefully and study Figures 1 and 2 before you begin to dissect. Identify structures to be dissected before you begin.*

CAUTION: *Always be careful with all sharp objects.*

1. With the dorsal side up, pin both ends of the worm to the wax in the dissecting pan.
2. With scissors, begin about 2 cm in front of the clitellum and cut forward through the body wall just to the left of the dorsal blood vessel. Use care to cut through only the body wall. See Figure 3.
3. Separate the edges of the cut. Observe the space between the body wall and the intestine. This is the body cavity or coelom.

Figure 3

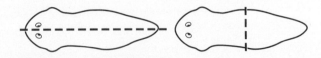

4. Observe the partitions between the segments. Use a dissecting needle to break these partitions. Then pin down the sides of the body wall.
5. Observe the tubelike digestive system. Identify the pharynx in segments 4 and 5. It is used to swallow food.
6. Follow the esophagus to segment 15.
7. Locate the large thin-walled crop. Food is stored in the crop until it is digested.
8. Locate the gizzard just behind the crop. Food is broken down by a grinding action in the gizzard here. The intestine extends from the gizzard to the anus. Digestion of food occurs in the intestine.
9. Each earthworm has both male and female reproductive organs. Alongside the esophagus in segments 9 and 10 are two pairs of seminal receptacles. The seminal receptacles receive sperm from another worm. In front of the receptacles in segments 10, 11, and 12 are seminal vesicles where sperm is stored.
10. Use a hand lens to find the small ovaries where eggs are produced. The ovaries are located under the seminal vesicles.
11. Locate the dorsal blood vessel. It carries blood to the heart-like structure, called the aortic arches. Carefully remove the white seminal vesicles from the left side of the body. Find the aortic arches, which branch from the dorsal blood vessel and pass around the esophagus.

Laboratory Activity 1 (continued)

These arches join the ventral blood vessel below the esophagus. These aortic arches contract and function as hearts. The ventral blood vessel carries blood toward the skin and intestine.

12. Use a hand lens to observe the small white tubes along each side of the digestive tract. These tubes are excretory organs called nephridia. They are found in all segments except the first three and the last. They remove the wastes from the body.

13. Find the double nerve ganglion, or brain, of the earthworm near segment 2. The brain connects with the ventral nerve cord, which extends the length of the body. The nerve cord is a white line on the ventral body wall.

14. **CAUTION:** *Give all dissected materials to your teacher for disposal. Always wash your hands after a dissection procedure.*

Data and Observations

List the organs found in each system in Table 1.

Table 1

Systems and Organs of an Earthworm	
System	**Organs**
1. Digestive	
2. Reproductive	
3. Circulatory	
4. Excretory	
5. Nervous	

Questions and Conclusions

1. How many setae were located on each segment?

_____

2. What is the function of the setae?

_____

3. Describe the function of the following organs:
   a. pharynx

_____

   b. crop

_____

   c. gizzard

_____

Laboratory Activity 1 (continued)

   d. aortic arches

_____

   e. dorsal blood vessel

_____

   f. ventral blood vessel

_____

   g. clitellum

_____

   h. nephridia

_____

   i. seminal vesicles

_____

   j. intestine

_____

   k. ganglia

_____

4. Why is it said that the earthworm has a "closed" circulatory system?

_____

Strategy Check

_____ Can you identify the external parts of an earthworm?

_____ Can you dissect an earthworm?

_____ Can you identify the internal organs and organ systems of an earthworm?

Grasshopper Anatomy

Chapter 8

A grasshopper is well adapted to its way of life. Its features are representative of the insect group. A grasshopper is large enough that its features can be seen easily.

Strategy

You will observe and identify the specialized body parts of the grasshopper.
You will examine and identify the internal and external structure of the grasshopper.

Materials

dissecting pan
grasshopper (preserved)
hand lens
forceps
dissecting scissors

Procedure

Part A—External Structure

1. Place the grasshopper in the dissecting pan. Locate the head, thorax, and abdomen. (See Figure 1.) Use your hand lens to observe the grasshopper carefully. As you observe, record your data in Data and Observations.

2. Observe the parts of the head. The grasshopper has two compound eyes and three simple eyes. The sensory parts located on the head are antennae.

3. Identify the mouth parts. (Refer to Figure 2.) With your forceps, remove the parts. The labrum is the hinged upper lip that is used to hold food. The mandibles are crushing jaws. The maxillae are used to chew and taste food. The labium is the broad, fat lower lip used to hold food while it is being chewed.

Figure 2

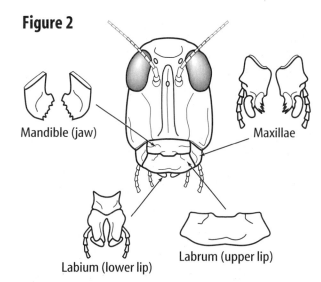

Mandible (jaw)   Maxillae
Labium (lower lip)   Labrum (upper lip)

Figure 1

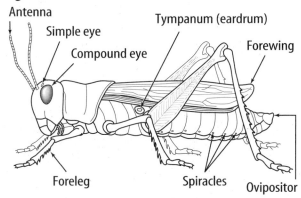

Antenna
Simple eye
Compound eye
Tympanum (eardrum)
Forewing
Foreleg   Spiracles   Ovipositor

4. Locate the eardrums or tympana, small drum-shaped structures on either side of the thorax.

5. All insects have six legs. In the grasshopper, the front pair is used for walking, climbing, and holding food. The middle legs are used for walking and climbing. The hind legs are large and enable the grasshopper to jump.

6. Locate the two pairs of wings.

7. Use the hand lens to look at the tiny openings along the abdomen. These are breathing pores called spiracles through which oxygen enters and carbon dioxide leaves.

8. A female grasshopper has a much longer abdomen than a male. It ends in a four-pointed tip, called an ovipositor, through which eggs are laid.

Laboratory Activity 2 (continued)

Figure 3

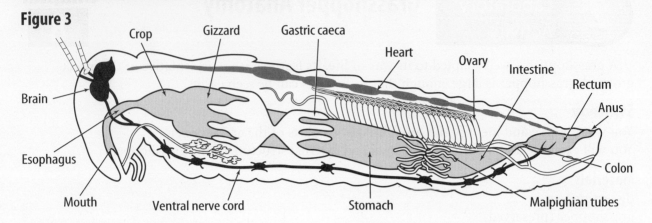

Brain, Crop, Gizzard, Gastric caeca, Heart, Ovary, Intestine, Rectum, Anus, Esophagus, Mouth, Ventral nerve cord, Stomach, Malpighian tubes, Colon

Part B—Internal Structure

1. Remove the three left legs. Insert the point of your scissors under the top surface of the last segment of the abdomen. Make a cut to the left of the mid-dorsal line. Be careful not to cut the organs underneath. In front of the thorax, cut down the left side to the bottom of the grasshopper. Cut down between the next to the last and last abdominal segments. **CAUTION:** *Always be careful with all sharp objects.*

2. Use your forceps to pull down the left side. Locate the large dorsal blood vessel.

3. Use your scissors to cut the muscles close to the exoskeleton. Locate the finely branched trachea leading to the spiracles.

4. Cut through the exoskeleton over the top of the head between the left antenna and left eye to the mouth. Remove the exoskeleton on the left side of the head. Find the dorsal ganglion or brain.

5. Cut away the tissue to show the digestive system. Refer to Figure 3 and identify the mouth, esophagus, crop, gizzard, and stomach. Note that the gizzard and stomach are separated by a narrow place. The digestive glands, called gastric caeca, that secrete enzymes into the stomach are attached here.

6. Another narrow place separates the stomach from the intestine. Malpighian tubes, which collect wastes from the blood, are located here.

7. Observe the colon, which enlarges to form the rectum. Wastes collect here before passing out the anus.

8. In the female, the ovary is located above the intestines. In the male, a series of whitish tubes, the testes, are located above the intestine.

9. **CAUTION:** *Give all dissected materials to your teacher for disposal. Always wash your hands after a dissection procedure.*

Laboratory Activity 2 (continued)

Data and Observations

1. What are the three sections of a grasshopper's body?

_____

_____

2. Record your observations of grasshopper body parts in Table 1. Complete the table by listing the function of each part.

Table 1

Body part	How many?	Function
1. Eyes		
2. Antennae		
3. Labrum		
4. Mandibles		
5. Maxillae		
6. Labium		
7. Eardrums		
8. Legs		
9. Wings		
10. Spiracles		
11. Ovipositor (if female)		
12. Digestive glands		
13. Tubules		
14. Rectum		

Questions and Conclusions

1. How is a grasshopper's mouth adapted for plant eating?

_____

_____

2. What is the difference between a grasshopper's skeleton and yours?

_____

_____

Laboratory Activity 2 (continued)

3. How is a grasshopper's digestive system different from yours?

_____

_____

4. How does a grasshopper's legs help it to survive?

_____

_____

_____

5. To which animal group does the grasshopper belong?

_____

6. How does a grasshopper breathe?

_____

_____

Strategy Check

_____ Can you observe and identify specialized parts of the grasshopper?

_____ Can you examine and identify the internal and external parts of the grasshopper?

LAB
1 Laboratory Activity

Fish Dissection

Most fish are bony fish—bass, cod, salmon, and halibut are good examples. Most bony fish are covered with smooth, slimy scales, have a swim bladder, and have well-developed fins. Humans depend on bony fish as a high-protein, low-fat food source.

Strategy

You will dissect a bony fish, locating the swim bladder and the gills.
You will determine the age of the fish using the rings of its scales.

Materials

whole preserved fish (perch or trout work well)
tray
scalpel
dissecting scissors
magnifying lens

Procedure

1. Put the fish on a clean tray. Note its shape, color, and size in the data table in the Data and Observations section.
2. Examine the gills. Describe them in the data table in the Data and Observations section.

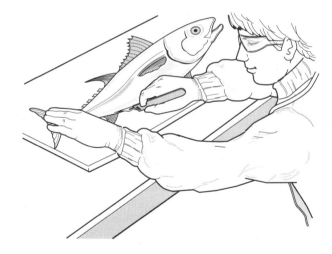

3. Insert the scalpel blade into the anus, or vent, of the fish. This is located just in front of the anal fin on the lower side of the fish.
4. Cut in a straight line along the fish's belly toward the head.
5. Use scissors to cut through the bones encountered along the midline. Keep cutting until you reach the area directly below the gills.
6. Now pull apart the two walls of the fish's body cavity to expose the internal organs.
7. The swim bladder is located roughly in the center of the fish. Pull the pinkish-red organs and tissue forward until you see the grayish-silver swim bladder.
8. Use the scalpel and scissors to remove the internal organs. This will allow better access to the swim bladder. Describe the bladder in the data table below.
9. Examine the scales of the fish. The number of rings on a scale tells you the age of the fish. Remove one scale and look at it with the magnifying lens. Count the rings on the scale to determine the age of the fish. Record this number in the data table on the next page.

Laboratory Activity 1 (continued)

Data and Observations

Fish Dissection Observations	
General description	1.
Description of gills	2.
Description of swim bladder	3.
Number of rings on scale	4.

Questions and Conclusions

1. Give a general description of the fish you dissected.

_____

_____

_____

2. How are the fish's gills designed for their function?

_____

_____

3. Describe how the air bladder differs from the other internal organs.

_____

_____

_____

4. Why do you think the swim bladder is located in the center of the fish?

_____

_____

_____

5. Describe the location of the fins on your fish.

_____

_____

_____

Laboratory Activity 1 (continued)

6. A bony fish maintains its depth in the water by adjusting the amount of gas inside its swim bladder. A fish's position in the water adjusts as the gas enters and leaves the swim bladder. Explain what will happen to the swim bladder of a fish swimming in very deep water.

_____

_____

_____

_____

Strategy Check

_____ Can you dissect a bony fish, locating the swim bladder and the gills?

_____ Can you determine the age of the fish using the rings of its scales?

Owl Pellets

The barn owl usually feeds on small mammals such as rodents, moles, and shrews. These mammals are swallowed whole. Some parts of the mammals dissolve in the owl's stomach. The indigestible parts, such as bones, hair, and feathers, are regurgitated in an owl pellet. You can find out what an owl eats by examining the owl pellet in this laboratory.

Strategy

You will dissect an owl pellet and identify animal skulls found in the owl pellet.
You will construct a chart of the numbers and kinds of prey eaten by owls.

Materials

plastic gloves
forceps
owl pellet
white sheet of paper
dissecting needle
field guide to small mammals

Procedure

1. Use the forceps to place the owl pellet on the white paper.
2. Break the owl pellet apart. Carefully separate the bones of the animals from the feather and fur.
3. Use the forceps and dissecting needle to clean skull bones. **CAUTION:** *Use sharp objects with care.*

4. Identify the skulls of the animals that the owl has eaten. You will need to use a field guide to small mammals. Record the number of skulls of different animals in Table 1.
5. Make a class record of the kinds and numbers of animals found in the owl pellets.

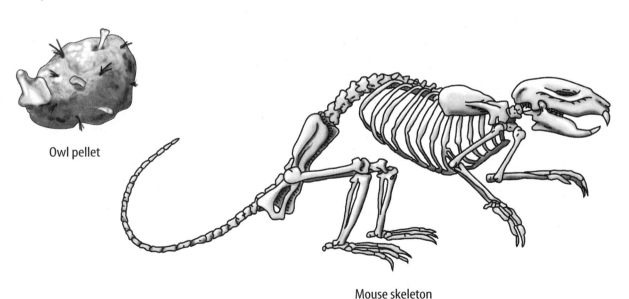

Owl pellet

Mouse skeleton

Laboratory Activity 2 (continued)

Data and Observations

Table 1

Animal	Number—individual	Number—class
Shrew		
Mole sparrow		
Vole		
Deer mouse		
Rat		
Other		
Total		

Questions and Conclusions

1. What was the outside covering of the owl pellet?

_____

_____

2. An owl regurgitates one pellet a day. How many animals did your owl eat in one day?

_____

3. What animals did you find in the owl pellet?

_____

4. What is the owl's role in the environment?

_____

_____

5. Is the owl a herbivore or a carnivore?

_____

6. Poisons found in the environment often accumulate in the bodies of small mammals. How would this affect the owl that preys on these animals?

_____

Strategy Check

_____ Did you dissect an owl pellet and identify animal skulls?

_____ Did you construct a chart of the kind and numbers of prey eaten by owls?

Root Structure and Functions

Roots hold a plant in the ground. They also absorb, store, and transport water and minerals. They have small threadlike side roots with root hairs that absorb water and minerals from the soil. Taproots, such as carrots, have a primary root that grows straight down into the soil. Taproots look very different from fibrous roots, such as grasses, which have many small roots branching out in different directions.

Strategy
You will examine a dissected carrot root.
You will label a diagram of a root and list the function of each part.

Materials
carrot sliced crosswise
carrot sliced lengthwise
hand lens

Procedure
1. Your teacher will prepare a crosswise slice of a carrot for you.
2. Hold the slice up to the light. Compare what you see with Figure 1 under Data and Observations.
3. Examine the lengthwise slice of the carrot. Use the hand lens. Look at both the inner and outer parts.
4. The outside layer of the root is the epidermis. Lateral roots grow from the epidermal cells and root hairs grow from them. Label the epidermis, lateral roots, and root hairs if all of these structures are present.

5. Inside the epidermis, you will find several layers of large, loosely packed cells that store food. This is the cortex. Food stored in the cortex can be used by other cells of the plant. Label the cortex.
6. Inside the cortex are tubelike cells from xylem vessels that carry water and minerals in the plant. Label the xylem cells.
7. Other tubelike cells inside the cortex carry food in the plant. These cells are called phloem cells. Label the phloem cells.

Data and Observations

Figure 1

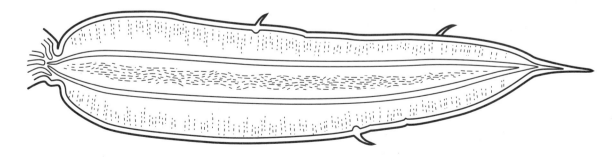

Laboratory Activity 1 (continued)

Questions and Conclusions

1. What type of root is the carrot?

_____

2. What is the function of the root hairs?

_____

_____

3. How many different kinds of cells did you see in the carrot slice?

_____

4. What is the name and function of the outer ring of cells?

_____

5. What is the green part at the top end of the carrot?

_____

6. What is the name and function of the thicker layer of cells next to the epidermis?

_____

7. What cells are found in the inner core?

_____

8. What is the function of these cells?

_____

_____

9. Why do you think taproots are used as food more often than fibrous roots?

_____

_____

_____

10. List some other food plants that have a taproot.

_____

_____

_____

Strategy Check

_____ Can you examine a carrot root?

_____ Can you identify the locations of each part of a root?

LAB 2 Laboratory Activity

Parts of a Fruit

Some of the plants we call vegetables are actually fruits. Fruits are formed inside flowers that have been pollinated and fertilized. After fertilization takes place, the petals fall off and the ovary begins to develop into the fruit.

Strategy

You will study the structure of typical fleshy and dry fruits.
You will examine several fruits and classify the fruits as fleshy or dry.

Materials

plum	peach	okra	pea in a pod	corn
tomato	peanut	olive	avocado	bean in a pod
apple	acorn	pear	sunflower seed	

Procedure

1. Read the following paragraphs and study the diagrams.

   The peach is a fleshy fruit. A fleshy fruit consists of a single ripened ovary with a soft, fleshy ovary wall when ripe. Three kinds of fleshy fruits are the drupe, pome, and the berry. The peach is a drupe. The exocarp is the covering of skin. The mesocarp is fleshy. The endocarp is hard and encloses the seed.

   The apple is a pome. The stem is the stalk by which the flower was attached. At the other end are the remains of the sepals, petals, and a ring of dried stamens. The thin skin is the epidermis. The fleshy part inside the skin developed from the receptacle, or flower stalk. The papery core is the ovary wall. Within the ovary are the seeds.

   The grape is a berry. The entire ovary is soft.

   Dry fruits have an ovary wall that is dry and brittle when ripe. They are classified as dehiscent or indehiscent. A dehiscent fruit splits along a definite seam when ripe. The bean is a dehiscent fruit called a legume. It splits along two seams.

2. Examine each of the fruits listed in Table 1 and determine if they are fleshy or dry. Determine the type of fruit (drupe, pome, or berry; dehiscent or indehiscent). Record your answers in the table.

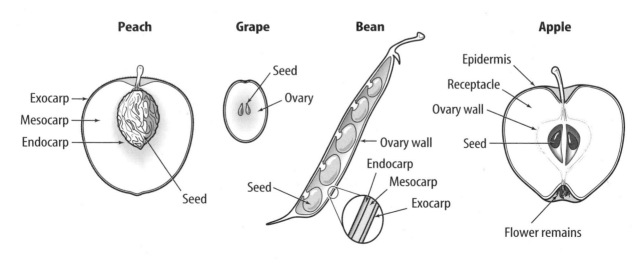

Laboratory Activity 2 (continued)

Data and Observations

Table 1

Fruit	Fleshy or dry	Type
1. Plum		
2. Tomato		
3. Apple		
4. Peach		
5. Peanut		
6. Acorn		
7. Okra		
8. Olive		
9. Pear		
10. Pea		
11. Avocado		
12. Sunflower		
13. Corn		
14. Bean		

Questions and Conclusions

1. What part of a flower becomes the fruit? _____

2. What part of a flower becomes the seed? _____

3. What are some fruits that we call vegetables? _____

4. What are some seeds that people eat? _____

5. From what part of the flower does a peach develop? _____

6. From what part of the flower does a grape develop? _____

Strategy Check

_____ Did you study the structure of fleshy and dry fruits?

_____ Did you examine several fruits and classify them as fleshy or dry?

Water Loss

A plant continually needs water to grow. According to some calculations, a corn plant needs a barrel of water to produce one ear of corn. Plants lose water through their leaves.

Strategy

You will observe water loss from a plant.
You will measure the amount of water used by a plant.

Materials

cork stoppers (prepared by teacher)
corn seedlings (about 4 days old)
plasticine (clay)
2 test tubes
water

metric ruler
tape (adhesive or masking)
labels
test-tube rack

Figure 1

a

b

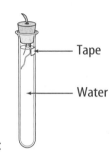

Tape

Water

c

Procedure

1. Place a young corn plant between the halves of a hollowed-out cork. See Figure 1a.
2. Carefully add plasticine around the stem of the corn and the stopper to form a tight seal. Do not break the stem. See Figure 1b.
3. Fill a test tube with water to about 2.5 cm from the top. Carefully insert the plant and stopper into the tube. If the roots of the corn plant are not in water, add more water to the tube until the roots are in water. **CAUTION:** *Do not force the stopper into the tube. Ask your teacher for help.*
4. Carefully add more plasticine to the cut edges of the top of the cork for a complete seal.
5. Place tape on the test tube so that the top edge marks the height of the water in the tube. See Figure 1c. Label the test tube with your name and the date.

6. Prepare a second test tube with cork halves but no corn seedling. Seal the bottom and top of the halves with plasticine. Add water to about 2.5 cm from the top.
7. Add tape and a label with your name and date. This will be the control tube.
8. Place both tubes in a test-tube rack where they will receive light.
9. Measure the total change in water level from the top edge of the tape each day for at least four days. Record your results in Table 1.

Laboratory Activity 1 (continued)

Data and Observations

Table 1

Total Change of Water Level (millimeters)		
Day	Tube with no corn	Tube with corn
1		
2		
3		
4		

Questions and Conclusions

1. Which tube lost the most water in four days?

_____

_____

2. What was the purpose of the control tube?

_____

_____

3. What evidence was there of water loss from the plant?

_____

_____

4. How do you know the water was not from the cork?

_____

_____

5. What is the process of water loss from a plant called?

_____

_____

Strategy Check

_____ Can you observe water loss from a plant?

_____ Can you measure the amount of water used by a plant?

Tropisms

Chapter 11

The response of a plant to a stimulus is called a tropism. The response of a plant to the stimulus of Earth's gravity is called gravitropism. The response to light is called phototropism. The response to water is called hydrotropism. Tropisms are controlled by chemicals called auxins.

Strategy

You will observe a plant's responses to light and gravity.
You will record your observations and determine how gravity and light affect root and stem growth.

Materials

3 corn seedlings
beaker of water
tape
4 shoe boxes
scissors
paper towel
4 straight pins
plastic bag
cardboard for mounting test tubes and seeds
4 radish seedlings growing in a container

cotton
3 test tubes
dropper
metric ruler
stapler
4 soaked corn seeds
petri dish

Figure 1

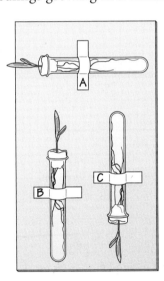

Procedure

Part A

1. Carefully wrap cotton around three corn seedlings. Dip each wrapped seedling into a beaker of water to wet the cotton.
2. Place one cotton-wrapped seedling into the mouth of each test tube. The cotton should fit snugly enough into the test tube so only the shoot of the seedling sticks out.

3. Tape the test tubes to the cardboard as shown in Figure 1. One test tube should be horizontal. Another test tube should be vertical with the shoot up. The third test tube should be vertical with the shoot down.
4. Stand the cardboard on a shelf where it will not be disturbed. Moisten the cotton each day using a dropper.
5. Observe the seedlings for one week. Record your observations in Table 1.

Part B

1. Label four shoe boxes A, B, C, and D. Cut a 3 × 8 cm rectangular hole in the side of Box A. Cut a 3 × 8 cm rectangular hole in the end of Box B. Cut a 3 × 8 cm hole in the top of Box C. Do not cut Box D. See Figure 2. **CAUTION:** *Always be careful when using scissors.*
2. Place a radish plant in each box. Then place the plants in a well-lighted area. Let the plants remain in the lighted area for one week.
3. Record your observations in Table 2 at the end of the week.

Figure 2

Laboratory Activity 2 (continued)

Part C

1. Cut a rectangular piece of cardboard 10 × 20 cm. Fold the cardboard in half. Staple a piece of paper towel to one side of the cardboard.

2. Position four soaked corn seeds in a line on the cardboard. Pin the seeds onto the cardboard so that the pointed end of one is down, one up, one left, and one right. Stand the cardboard in a shallow dish of water so that the seeds are all about the same distance from the water. See Figure 3.

3. Cover the cardboard and dish with a plastic bag.

4. Observe the root and stem growth of each seed for one week. Record your final observations in Table 3.

Figure 3

Data and Observations

Table 1

Test tube	In what direction does the seedling stem grow?	In what direction does the seedling root grow?
A		
B		
C		

Table 2

Radish plant	Observations
A	
B	
C	
D	

Laboratory Activity 2 (continued)

Table 3

Position of corn seed point	In what direction does the stem grow?	In what direction does the root grow?
Down		
Up		
Left		
Right		

Questions and Conclusions

1. Did any of the corn seedlings grow without bending?

   _____

   If so, which ones?

   _____

2. Did any of the corn seedlings bend as they grew?

   _____

   If so, which ones?

   _____

3. Which way did the roots grow?

   _____

4. Which way did the stems grow?

   _____

5. What affects the direction of root growth in this activity?

   _____

   Is this effect positive or negative?

   _____

6. What affects the direction of stem growth?

   _____

   Is this effect positive or negative?

   _____

7. In what direction did the stems of the radish plant bend?

   _____

Laboratory Activity 2 (continued)

8. From which end of the corn seeds did the roots grow?

9. From which end of the corn seeds did the shoots grow?

10. Did the roots of all the seeds turn in one direction?

If so, what was the direction?

11. Did the shoots of all four seeds turn in one direction?

If so, what was the direction?

12. To what stimulus did the corn roots respond?

Was the response positive or negative?

13. To what stimulus did the corn shoots respond?

Was the response positive or negative?

14. What effect does gravity have on root growth?

15. What effect does gravity have on stem growth?

16. What effect does light have on stem growth?

Strategy Check

_____ Did you observe plant responses to light and gravity?

_____ Did you record your observations and determine how gravity and light affect root and stem growth?

LAB 1 Laboratory Activity

Modeling Cell Division in Early Development

Chapter 12

Every person starts out as a single cell. Cell division is responsible for the development of a baby from the single cell. As the single cell begins developing, cell division results in exponential growth in the number of cells present. Exponential growth is growth that occurs at an ever-increasing rate. On a graph, exponential growth is represented by a J-shaped curve.

Strategy

You will model how cell division results in exponential growth in the number of cells in a developing human.

You will determine why exponential growth cannot continue indefinitely during human development.

You will infer why uncontrolled cell division, which occurs in cancer, can be so harmful to human health.

Materials

uncooked rice
paper cups (11)
graph paper

Procedure

1. Obtain a container of uncooked rice from your teacher. Each grain of rice represents one human cell.

2. Place one grain of rice in a paper cup. This grain of rice represents the single cell that results when sperm and egg unite.

3. Label paper cups 1 through 10, and place them in a row next to the cup containing the original cell. During the first 10 cell divisions, the cells in the developing human all have the same cell cycle length.

4. Place two grains of rice into cup 1 to represent the number of cells present after the original cell undergoes the first round of mitosis. Record the number *2* in the table in the Data and Observations section.

5. Place grains of rice into cup 2 to represent the number of cells that will be present after the second round of mitosis. Record the number of cells in your data table.

6. Repeat step 5 for cups 3 through 10.

7. Using your data and graph paper, make a line graph that shows the growth in the numbers of cells. Label the *x*-axis *Number of cell divisions* and the *y*-axis *Number of cells.*

Laboratory Activity 1 (continued)

Data and Observations

Growth in Cell Number Due to Mitosis			
Number of mitotic divisions	Resulting number of cells	Number of mitotic divisions	Resulting number of cells
1		6	
2		7	
3		8	
4		9	
5		10	

Questions and Conclusions

1. Initially all of the cells in a developing human have the same cell-cycle length. After the eleventh round of mitosis, groups of cells begin to have different cell-cycle lengths. What step of the cell cycle is likely to be longer in cells with a longer cell cycle?

   _____

2. Could the type of growth you modeled with grains of rice continue indefinitely in a developing human? Explain your answer.

   _____

   _____

3. Cancer results from uncontrolled cell division. Using your results from this activity, infer why cancer can have such a serious effect on human health.

   _____

   _____

Strategy Check

_____ Can you model how cell division results in exponential growth?

_____ Can you determine why exponential growth cannot continue indefinitely?

_____ Can you infer why uncontrolled cell division can be harmful to human health?

Examining Models of Chromosomes

Chapter 12

Models of the chromosomes of the imaginary Leksak bird can be found at the end of this activity. The dark bands on these chromosome models are genes. Most cells in this bird's body contain the same number and type of chromosomes. The importance of genes to all living things, and to the Leksak bird as well, is that they control all inherited traits. Chromosomes are important because they are the carriers of these genes.

Strategy

You will cut out and pair chromosome models of the Leksak bird.
You will determine what type of change occurs in the number of chromosomes when a cell divides by mitosis and meiosis.

Materials

scissors

Procedure/Data and Observations

1. Cut out each chromosome model in Figure 1.
2. Fold each paper model in half along dotted lines.
3. Match in pairs as many chromosome models as possible. A chromosome pair must match in length as well as in number and location of genes. The lines on the chromosome models represent genes.
4. Answer questions 1 through 4 in Questions and Conclusions before proceeding further.
5. Cut each chromosome model in half along the dotted line. Make two piles of chromosome halves. Put one half of each chromosome in one pile and the other half in the second pile.
6. Compare the chromosomes in the first pile with those in the second pile.

7. Before proceeding, answer questions 5 and 6 in Questions and Conclusions.
8. Place all identical chromosome models together in separate groups. You should have six groups of models.
9. Take a group of matched chromosomes and separate them into four piles. Take a second group of matched chromosomes and place one chromosome from the group into each of the four piles.
10. Continue this sorting until all chromosome models, including the unmatched chromosome models, have been separated into the four piles. Each pile of chromosome models represents a sex cell.

Cell division includes a process called mitosis that occurs in most living things. During mitosis, one cell divides to produce two cells. The cutting of each chromosome model and separating them into two piles is similar to what happens in a living cell during cell division. The two piles of chromosome models represent two new cells. (Each chromosome duplicates itself and the two halves then separate.)

A process called meiosis occurs in some living things. During meiosis, one diploid cell divides to produce four haploid cells. Each new cell produced by this process is called a sex cell (egg or sperm).

Laboratory Activity 2 (continued)

Questions and Conclusions

1. How many chromosomes can be found in each of the Leksak bird's cells?

   _____

2. How many matched pairs of chromosomes are there in each cell?

   _____

3. How many unmatched chromosomes are there in each cell?

   _____

4. Do the genes on each matched pair of chromosomes also match?

   _____

5. After separating the chromosome model halves into two piles, how many models are found in each pile?

   _____

6. How many chromosomes are found in Leksak sex cells?

   _____

7. Do any chromosomes match one another in a sex cell?

   _____

8. Male Leksak birds have six matched pairs of chromosomes and one unmatched pair of chromosomes. Female Leksak birds have seven matched pairs of chromosomes. Were the chromosomes in our bird taken from a male or a female?

   _____

9. Are all cells produced by mitosis exactly alike, chromosome for chromosome? Gene for gene? Explain.

   _____

   _____

10. How does the number of chromosomes in sex cells compare to the number of chromosomes in cells formed during mitosis?

    _____

    _____

11. Explain two ways in which sex cells differ from all other cells.

    _____

Strategy Check

_____ Did you cut out and match in pairs the chromosome models of the Leksak bird?

_____ Did you determine the types of changes that occur in the number of chromosomes when a cell undergoes mitosis or meiosis?

Laboratory Activity 2 (continued)

Figure 1

Models of chromosomes for the imaginary Leksak bird after duplication in the interphase period of the cell cycle.

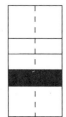

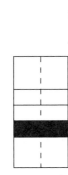

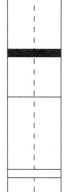

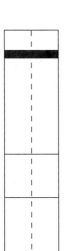
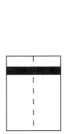

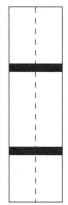

Genetic Traits

Have you ever been told you look like your parents? Parents pass genes that determine physical features to their children. These physical features are called genetic traits. Children receive half of their genes from each parent. The genes of one parent may be dominant over the genes of the other parent. A child usually looks most like the parent who supplies the most dominant genes.

Strategy

You will examine some of your genetic traits.
You will examine your parents for the same genetic traits.
You will compare how similar or different you and your parents are.

Materials

pencil

Procedure

1. Work with a partner during this activity. Complete the column marked "You" in Table 1 in Data and Observations for each of the genetic traits listed. Ask your partner to help you describe the traits you cannot see. Refer to Figure 1 for an explanation of traits you may not be familiar with.
2. Optional: Take the table home and complete it for each of your parents.

Figure 1

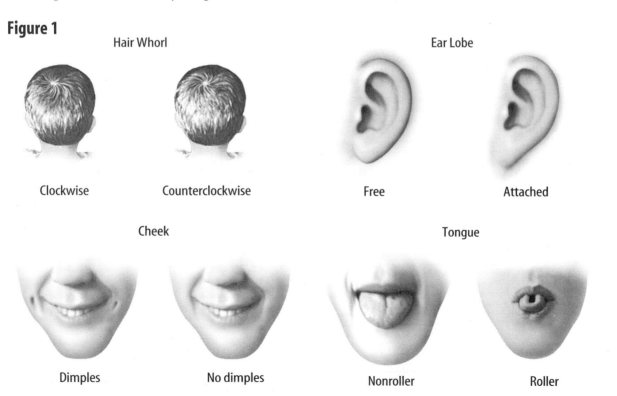

| Hair Whorl | | Ear Lobe | |

Clockwise   Counterclockwise   Free   Attached

Cheek   Tongue

Dimples   No dimples   Nonroller   Roller

Laboratory Activity 1 (continued)

Data and Observations

Record your results in the table.

Table 1

Trait	Description	You	Father	Mother
Handedness	Left or right			
Sight	Nearsighted or normal			
Eye color	Blue or not blue			
Dimples*	Yes or no			
Freckles	Present or absent			
Hair whorl*	Clockwise or counterclockwise			
Earlobe*	Free or attached			
Tongue*	Roller or nonroller			

* See Figure 1.

Questions and Conclusions

1. How many traits do you and your mother share?

   _____

   You and your father?

   _____

2. How many traits do you share with both parents?

   _____

3. List all traits that you show but are not shown by either parent.

   _____

4. How might it be possible to show a trait when both parents do not show it?

   _____

5. What proof do you have that all of your genes did not come from only one parent?

   _____

Strategy Check

_____ Can you identify some genetic traits?

_____ Can you count how many traits are the same for each parent and you?

_____ Can you make any conclusions about the traits you received from each parent?

50:50 Chances

The chance of a flipped coin landing with the "heads" side up rather than the "tails" side is 50:50. Does that mean that for every two times a coin if flipped, heads will turn up once and tails will turn up once? The chance of a boy rather than a girl being born in a family is also 50:50. Does that mean that in a family with six children, three are boys and three are girls? You know the answer to both of these questions is no. What is the value, then, of saying the chances are 50:50?

Strategy

You will compare the chances of a boy or girl being born with the chances of a flipped coin landing on one side or the other.

You will flip a coin six times to represent the sexes of children in one family.

You will record your results and compare the sexes of the children in 15 families.

Materials

coin

Procedure

1. Let the heads side of the coin represent girls. Let the tails side represent boys. Flip the coin six times. How many times did girls turn up? How many times did boys turn up? Record these totals in the columns.

2. Continue to flip the coin until you have a total of 15 groups of six flips each.

Data and Observations

Table 1

Group	1	2	3	4	5	6	7	8	9	10	11	12	13	14	15
Girls (heads)															
Boys (tails)															

1. Use slash marks / to complete Table 2 using the data recorded in Table 1 for each group of six flips.

Laboratory Activity 2 (continued)

Table 2

Possible combinations	6 girls 0 boys	5 girls 1 boy	4 girls 2 boys	3 girls 3 boys	2 girls 4 boys	1 girl 5 boys	0 girls 6 boys
Number of combinations							

Questions and Conclusions

1. Why can you use coin flips to represent sex combinations that may occur in families?

   _____

2. According to your results, is it possible to have a family of exactly three boys and three girls?

   _____

   Do you know any family where there are exactly three boys and three girls?

   _____

3. According to your results, is it possible to have a family of six children where the ratio of boys to girls is not exactly 50:50? _____

   Do you know of actual families where this is true? _____

4. According to your results, which combination of boys and girls occurred the most often?

   _____

   Does this agree with what you had expected? _____

5. Explain how one can make a statement that you expect three boys and three girls in every family of six children, but yet you may not get this ratio in an actual family.

   _____

6. Out of 90 total children (coins) counted, how many were males? _____ Females? _____

   Is your answer close to half boys and half girls? _____ Explain.

   _____

7. In a single family, the ratio may or may not be half boys and half girls. When do you begin to show that an equal number of boys and girls occurs in families?

   _____

Strategy Check

_____ Can you compare the chance of a boy or girl being born with the chance of a coin landing on one side or the other?

_____ Can you compare the sexes of the children in 15 families by flipping a coin?

_____ Can you explain how numbers, such as 50:50, can be used to show the likelihood of an occurrence?

Heart Structure

LAB 1 Laboratory Activity

Can you name the part of your body that is a muscle, works on its own without any reminder from you, pushes about five liters of liquid through your body each minute, relaxes for only about half a second, and squeezes or contracts 70 to 100 times a minute? The organ described is the human heart.

Strategy

You will observe the outside and inside of a cow or sheep heart to locate and label the parts of a heart.

You will study the direction of blood flow through the heart.

You will review the condition of blood on the right side of the heart as compared with the blood on the left side. Discuss side reversal in detail with the class to avoid confusion.

Materials

2 colored pencils (red and blue)
dissecting pan
dissecting probe
heart (sheep or cow)
*narrow tongue depressors
*coffee stirrers (alternative)

Procedure

Part A—Outside of Heart

1. Position your sheep or cow heart in a dissecting pan so that it matches Figure 1. **CAUTION:** *Wash hands thoroughly after handling heart.*
   NOTE: Use the description below and the directions of arrows in Figure 2 to help locate each part of the heart. Use Figure 2 to label each part as you identify it.

2. The *superior and inferior vena cava* returns blood to the right side of the heart from body organs. Locate and label the *superior and inferior vena cava.* The pulmonary vein returns blood to the left side of the heart from the lungs. Locate and label the *pulmonary vein.*

3. Blood in veins enters the right and left atrium, two small chambers at the top of the heart. Locate and label the *right atrium and left atrium.*

4. Pumping action of the heart squeezes blood from the atria into the right and left ventricles, two large chambers at the bottom of the heart. Locate and label the *right ventricle and left ventricle.*

Figure 1

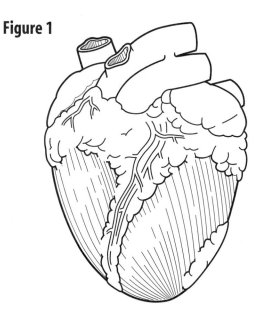

5. Pumping action of the heart squeezes blood from the two ventricles. Blood leaves the heart on the left side by way of an artery called the *aorta.* Locate and label the aorta, which carries blood to all body parts. Blood leaves the heart on the right side by way of another artery, the pulmonary artery. Locate and label the *pulmonary artery,* which carries blood to the lungs.

Laboratory Activity 1 (continued)

Figure 2

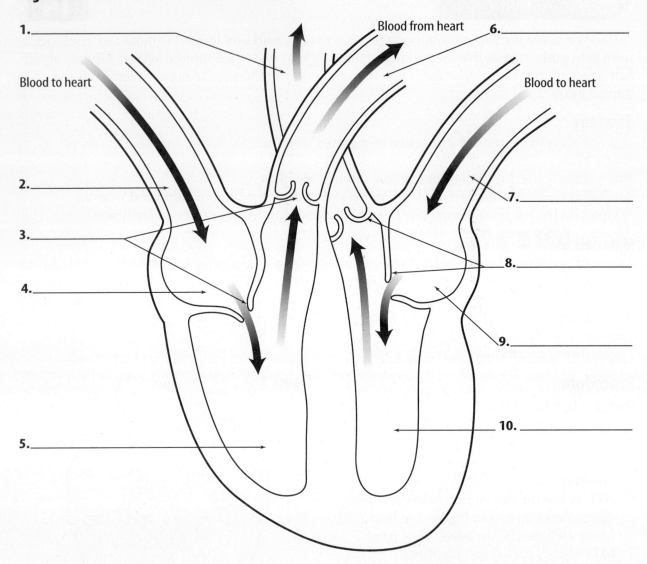

1. _____

Blood to heart

2. _____

3. _____

4. _____

5. _____

Blood from heart

6. _____

Blood to heart

7. _____

8. _____

9. _____

10. _____

Part B—Inside of Heart

1. Your teacher will slice open the heart with a scalpel.
2. Note the thickness of the muscle that makes up the left and right ventricles.
3. Locate and label the *heart valves* between atria and ventricles. Valves keep blood flowing in one direction.
4. Locate and label the valves where the pulmonary artery and aorta are joined to the heart.

Part C—Condition of Blood in Heart

1. Use a blue pencil to color in the spaces on Figure 2 to show where *deoxygenated blood* would be. Blood returning to or pumped from the right side of the heart is deoxygenated. This means that the amount of oxygen in the blood is low.
2. Use a red pencil to color in spaces to show where oxygenated blood would be. Oxygenated blood contains a large amount of oxygen. Those vessels returning to or leaving the left side of the heart carry *oxygenated blood*.

Laboratory Activity 1 (continued)

Data and Observations

1. Label and color Figure 2 as instructed in the Procedure. **NOTE:** Notice that Figure 2 shows the left and right sides of the heart reversed. The diagram actually shows the position of the heart in a person as it would appear if you were facing that person whose heart is shown.
2. Complete Table 1. Use the words *oxygenated* or *deoxygenated* to describe the condition of the blood in each part. (See Part C of the Procedure.)

Table 1

Part	Right side	Left side
Atrium		
Ventricle		
Vena cava		
Aorta		
Pulmonary vein		
Pulmonary artery		

Questions and Conclusions

1. To what part of the body is blood pumped as it passes through the pulmonary artery?

   _____

2. From what part of the body is blood being returned to the heart as it passes through the pulmonary veins? Through the vena cava?

   _____

   _____

3. If blood leaves the right side of the heart deoxygenated and returns to the left side oxygenated, what gas has been added to the blood? Through what organ must the blood pass in order to change in this way?

   _____

   _____

   _____

4. Explain why the muscle of the left ventricle is thicker than the muscle of the right ventricle.

   _____

   _____

5. Explain the function of the heart valves.

   _____

Laboratory Activity 1 (continued)

6. List in order those parts that determine the direction of blood flow through the heart. Start with the vena cava and include the following: left atrium, right atrium, left ventricle, right ventricle, pulmonary artery, pulmonary vein, aorta.

_____

_____

_____

7. Use the data in the Data and Observations section to explain the condition of all blood in
   a. the heart's right side.

_____

_____

   b. the heart's left side.

_____

_____

Strategy Check

_____ Can you locate and properly label the following parts of the heart: vena cava, right atrium, left atrium, pulmonary artery, pulmonary vein, left ventricle, right ventricle, aorta?

_____ Can you rearrange the above parts in proper order starting with the vena cava to show the direction of blood flow through the heart?

_____ Can you compare the condition of the blood on the right side of the heart to the blood on the left side?

Laboratory Activity

Blood Pressure

The main blood vessels of the body are the arteries and the veins. The heart pumps blood to all parts of the body by way of arteries. Veins carry blood back to the heart. Blood within your blood vessels is under pressure. Do arteries and veins have the same blood pressure?

Strategy

You will build an artificial heart and blood vessels with a plastic squeeze bottle and glass and rubber tubing.

You will measure and record the distance that water squirts from the glass tube and rubber tube.

You will compare the distance water squirts from each tube to the softness of the tubes.

Materials

food coloring (red)
2 glass tubes, 20 cm long and 5 cm long, 5-mm inside diameter, inserted in a rubber stopper (2-hole) by your teacher
meterstick
rubber tube, 18 cm long, 5-mm inside diameter
squeeze bottle
wash pan

Figure 1

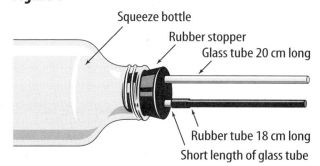

Squeeze bottle
Rubber stopper
Glass tube 20 cm long
Rubber tube 18 cm long
Short length of glass tube

Procedure

1. Fill a squeeze bottle with water. Add several drops of red food coloring to the water and shake gently.
2. Put the rubber stopper, with tubes attached, into the squeeze bottle opening. The stopper should fit tightly.
3. Rest a meterstick lengthwise on the edges of a washpan. Hold the rubber tube on one edge of the washpan. The rubber tube should be level with the glass tube. See Figure 2.

4. While a classmate squeezes the bottle, determine how far the water stream from each tube travels. Record your result in Table 1.
5. Refill the bottle before each new trial and repeat steps 3 and 4 three more times. Again record the results in the table.

Figure 2

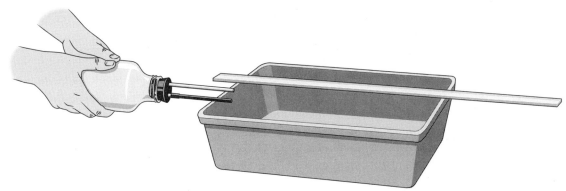

Laboratory Activity 2 (continued)

Data and Observations

1. Record your results in Table 1. Use centimeter units.

Table 1

Trial	1	2	3	4	Average
1. Glass tube					
2. Rubber tube					

2. Calculate the average distance water travels for each tube. Record the average in the table.

Questions and Conclusions

1. The higher the pressure in a tube, the farther water will travel when it comes out of the tube. In which tube was water pressure higher? In which tube was water pressure lower?

_____

_____

2. Veins are soft and flexible, while arteries are tougher and less flexible. Which tube corresponds to arteries? Which tube corresponds to veins?

_____

_____

3. Using your results, compare blood pressure in arteries to blood pressure in veins.

_____

_____

4. What part of your body can be compared to the squeeze bottle? The water?

_____

_____

Laboratory Activity 2 (continued)

Blood pressure is described by measuring two events: (**a**) Systolic pressure—pressure when the ventricles of the heart contract and push blood into arteries (**b**) Diastolic pressure—pressure when the ventricles relax and blood in the arteries is not being pushed.

Blood pressure is a comparison of systolic to diastolic numbers. Figure 3 shows blood pressure measured in mm of mercury compared with age in years. For example, the systolic pressure for a 10-year-old child is 100 mm of mercury. The diastolic pressure for this child is 70 mm of mercury.

Figure 3

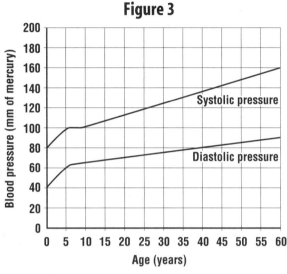

5. **a.** What is the systolic pressure for a 20-year-old person? _____

   b. What is the diastolic pressure for a 20-year-old person? _____

6. From the graph, determine the blood pressure for the following ages: (list systolic, then diastolic.)

   a. 15 years old _____

   _____

   b. 30 years old _____

   _____

   c. 40 years old _____

   _____

7. **a.** How much change occurs in systolic pressure from age 0 to 60?

   _____

   b. How much change occurs in diastolic pressure from age 0 to 60?

   _____

Laboratory Activity 2 (continued)

8. a. Does systolic blood pressure change more from age 0 to 20 than from age 20 to 60?

_____

9. a. At what age is there the greatest difference between systolic pressure and diastolic pressure?

_____

b. What is the blood pressure at this age? _____

_____

10. The age of a person with a systolic pressure of 116 and diastolic pressure of 75 should be close to what?

_____

A person is said to have high blood pressure if systolic and diastolic pressures are higher than normal. A person is said to have a low blood pressure if systolic and diastolic pressure are lower than normal. Record if the following people have *high, low,* or *normal* blood pressure by comparing the pressure in Table 2 with those in the graph in Figure 3.

Table 2

Blood Pressure			
Age	Systolic	Diastolic	Pressure
45	140	83	**11.**
30	130	85	**12.**
60	140	80	**13.**

Strategy Check

_____ Can you build an artificial heart and blood vessels?

_____ Can you determine which tube, glass or rubber, allows the water to squirt out farther when the bottle is squeezed?

_____ Can you correlate the distance water squirts to the softness of the rubber and glass tubes?

How does breathing occur?

Chapter 15

If you have ever tried to hold your breath, you know that breathing is automatic. Breathing is moving air into and out of the lungs. Taking in air is called inhalation. Letting out air is called exhalation. Your ribs and chest help with breathing. A muscle called the diaphragm also helps by contracting as you inhale and relaxing as you exhale.

Strategy

You will compare a model of the human chest to a human chest.
You will use the model to show how the diaphragm and chest help inhalation and exhalation.

Materials

model of the human chest

Procedure

Part A—Model Parts and How They Work

1. Obtain a model of the human chest from your teacher.
2. Using Figure 1 as a reference, push up gently on the rubber sheet and note the water level change in the tube. Record the water level changes for both sides of the tube in Table 1.
3. Pull down gently on the rubber sheet and note the water level change in the tube. Record your observations in Table 1.

Part B—Comparing Your Model with the Human Chest

Compare Figures 1 and 2. Match the parts of the model (Figure 1) with the parts of the human chest (Figure 2) in Table 2.

Part C—Comparing Your Model with the Human Chest

1. Gently push up on the rubber sheet of the model. Record your observations in Table 3. Note that the diaphragm is in a relaxed condition when it pushes up in your body.
2. Gently push down on the rubber sheet and record your observations in Table 3. Note that the diaphragm is in a contracted condition when it pulls down in your body.

Figure 1

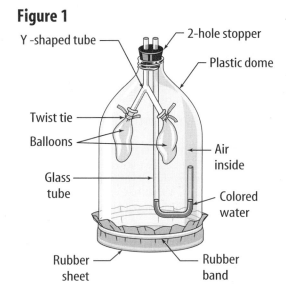

Figure 2

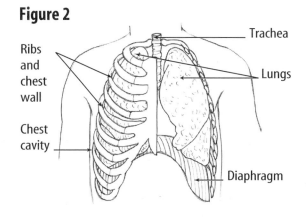

Laboratory Activity 1 (continued)

Part D—Comparing Your Model with the Human Chest

1. Gently squeeze in the sides of the bottom of the plastic dome (chest wall). Record your observations in Table 4. Note that the chest wall and the ribs in Figure 3A move down slightly when the human chest wall moves in.

2. Gently squeeze in the sides at the bottom of the plastic dome, and then let go. Record your observations in Table 4. Note that the chest wall and the ribs in Figure 3B move slightly up when the human chest wall moves out and that the size of the chest cavity gets larger.

Figure 3

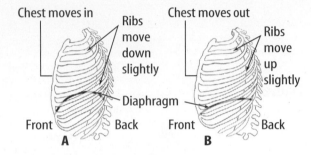

Chest moves in — Ribs move down slightly — Diaphragm — Front — Back — **A**

Chest moves out — Ribs move up slightly — Front — Back — **B**

Data and Observations

Table 1

Water Levels in the Chest Model				
Rubber sheet	Water level on long side	Water level on short side	Change in inside air pressure	Air pressure in model
1. Pushed up				
2. Pulled down				

Table 2

Identifying Model Parts	
Model parts	Parts of the human chest
1. Balloons	
2. Rubber sheet	
3. Y-shaped tube	
4. Air inside dome	
5. Plastic sides of dome	

Laboratory Activity 1 (continued)

Table 3

The Movement of the Diaphragm During Breathing						
Rubber sheet	Diaphragm condition (relaxed/ contracted)	Diaphragm position (up/down)	Tube side in which water rises (long/short)	Inside air pressure (high/low)	Balloons (air sacs) (empty/fill)	Person breathing (exhale/ inhale)
1. Pushed up						
2. Pulled down						

Table 4

The Movement of the Chest During Breathing		
	Chest wall pushed in	Chest wall back to original shape
1. Tube side in which water rises (long/short)		
2. Inside air pressure (falls/rises)		
3. Air pressure (high/low)		
4. Rib cage movement (up/down)		
5. Chest cavity size (large/small)		
6. Balloons or air sacs (empty/fill)		
7. Person breathing (exhale/inhale)		

Laboratory Activity 1 (continued)

Questions and Conclusions

Directions: *Complete the following summary table based on the results of your activities.*

Inhalation and Exhalation		
	Inhalation	Exhalation
1. Diaphragm pulled up or down?		
2. Diaphragm relaxed or contracted?		
3. Chest wall pushed in or out?		
4. Ribs pulled up or down?		
5. Air pressure in chest high or low?		
6. Pressure does or does not squeeze air sacs?		
7. Chest cavity size increases or decreases?		
8. Lungs filling or emptying?		
9. Breathing in or out?		

Strategy Check

_____ Can you compare the model to a human chest?

_____ Can you use the model to show how the diaphragm and chest wall help inhalation and exhalation?

Lung Capacity

LAB 2 Laboratory Activity

Chapter 15

Take a deep breath, then let it out. Every day you breathe in and out thousands of times. How much air do you breathe when you take a deep breath? The amount of air your lungs can hold is the capacity of your lungs. You can determine your lung capacity.

Strategy

You will measure the amount of air in your lungs.
You will determine your average lung capacity.

Materials

balloon (round)
metric ruler

Procedure

1. Stretch a balloon several times. Then take a deep breath and blow into the balloon. Exhale as much air as possible.
2. When you take the balloon away from your mouth, hold the open end tightly so that no air escapes. Resume normal breathing.
3. Measure the air-filled balloon's diameter by placing it next to a ruler as shown in Figure 1. Record the diameter of the balloon in Table 1 in Data and Observations.
4. Repeat steps 1–3 four more times. Record the results in Data and Observations.

5. The diameter of your balloon does not give you your lung capacity. To change the diameter of the balloon to liters (the metric unit for volume), you must use a graph. Locate your balloon diameter for Trial 1 along the bottom axis of the graph in Figure 2. Read up to the curved dark line, then across to locate your lung capacity. Record your lung capacity for all trials.
6. Total your results by adding each column of numbers in Table 1. Find the average by dividing each total by the number of trials.

Figure 1

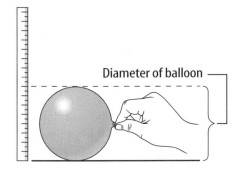

Diameter of balloon

Figure 2

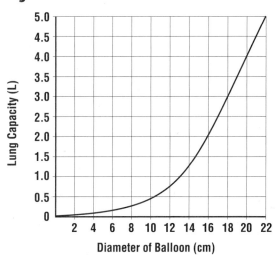

Laboratory Activity 2 (continued)

Data and Observations

Table 1

Trial	Your balloon diameter (cm)	Capacity (L)
1		
2		
3		
4		
5		
Total		
Average		

Questions and Conclusions

1. What is meant by the term *lung capacity*?

   _____

2. Why was it necessary to change the balloon diameter to liters when finding lung capacity?

   _____

3. How does your lung capacity differ from those of other students in your class?

   _____

4. A person with a lung capacity of 3 L could blow a balloon to what diameter? (Refer to Figure 2.)

5. Why might it be important to know a person's lung capacity?

   _____

   _____

Strategy Check

_____ Can you measure the amount of air in your lungs?

_____ Can you determine your average lung capacity?

Testing for Carbohydrates

Chapter 16

Carbohydrates provide energy for the body. Your body needs more carbohydrates than fats and proteins each day. Foods that contain starch and foods that contain sugar are sources of carbohydrates.

Strategy

You will test foods for starch by using iodine solution.

You will test foods for sugar by using sugar test tablets.

You will use your test results to determine which foods are sources of carbohydrates.

Materials

12 test tubes (18 × 150-mm)	egg white (hard-boiled)	honey
test-tube rack	potato (cooked)	milk
water	iodine in dropper bottle	molasses
starch	labels	forceps
bread	glucose	sugar test tablets
rice (cooked)	syrup	

Procedure

CAUTION: *Do not taste, eat, or drink any materials used in the lab.*

CAUTION: *Inform your teacher if you come in contact with any chemicals.*

1. Label six test tubes 1 through 6. Place them in a test-tube rack.

2. Fill the test tubes to about 1 cm with the following.

1—Water	4—Rice
2—Starch	5—Egg White
3—Bread	6—Potato

3. Add 5 drops of iodine to test tubes 1–6. **CAUTION:** *Iodine is poisonous. Do not inhale iodine fumes. Do not allow iodine to get on your hands. Wash immediately if iodine comes in contact with your skin. Inform your teacher.* Examine the color. A blue-black color means that starch is present. Record the colors in Table 1. (See Data and Observations.)

4. Label the remaining test tubes 7 through 12. Place them in a test-tube rack.

5. Fill these test tubes to a depth of about 1 cm with the following:

7—Water	10—Honey
8—Glucose	11—Milk
9—Syrup	12—Molasses

6. Use forceps to add one sugar test tablet each to test tubes 7–12. **CAUTION:** *Sugar tablets are poisonous. DO NOT touch the tablet with your fingers. Wash hands immediately if sugar test tablets or solution containing them come in contact with your skin. The test tubes will get hot as the tablets dissolve. Do not remove the test tubes from the test tube rack. DO NOT TOUCH.*

7. Observe the color of each of the five tubes. Green, yellow, or orange color means that sugar is present. Record the colors in Table 2.

Laboratory Activity 1 (continued)

Data and Observations

Table 1

Starch Test				
Test Tube	Contents	Color after adding iodine	Starch present? (yes or no)	Carbohydrate? (yes or no)
1				
2				
3				
4				
5				
6				

Table 2

Sugar Test				
Test Tube	Contents	Color after adding sugar test tablet	Sugar present? (yes or no)	Carbohydrate? (yes or no)
7				
8				
9				
10				
11				
12				

Questions and Conclusions

1. Which foods tested showed starch present?

_____

Explain how you know.

_____

_____

Laboratory Activity 1 (continued)

2. Which foods tested showed sugar present?

_____

Explain how you know.

_____

3. Why was water tested for both starch and sugar?

_____

_____

4. Why was starch tested for starch?

_____

_____

5. Why was glucose tested for sugar?

_____

_____

6. Which foods are carbohydrates?

_____

_____

7. Explain how starch and sugar are related.

_____

_____

Strategy Check

_____ Can you test foods for starch by using iodine solution?

_____ Can you test foods for sugar by using test tablets?

_____ Can you use the test results to determine which foods are sources of carbohydrates?

LAB 2 Laboratory Activity — Digestion of Fats

Chapter 16

Did you know that a chemical compound in your liver performs a job similar to your teeth? It helps to break down fats and oils so that digestion can occur more easily. Eventually, the fat and oil are changed into a form that can be used by the body for energy.

Strategy

You will find out if fats mix with water.
You will determine if chemicals help to mix fats with water.
You will determine what substances can best break down vegetable oil (fat).
You will indicate how this action is related to the human digestive system.

Materials

5 test tubes (18 × 150-mm)	5 droppers	lemon juice
5 stoppers to fit test tubes	metric ruler	liquid detergent
tape	vegetable oil	newspaper
test-tube rack	alcohol	
water	bile (5% solution)	

Procedure

1. Use tape to label five test tubes 1, 2, 3, 4, and 5. Place them in a test-tube rack.

2. Add water to a height of 4 cm to each test tube.

3. With a dropper, place 4 drops of vegetable oil into each test tube. Observe whether the oil remains on the top or bottom of the water. Record your observations. (See Data and Observations.) Record if the line between the oil and water is sharp or fuzzy.

4. Add the following to each test tube using a different dropper with each. **CAUTION:** *Bile solution stains.*
   Tube 1—nothing more
   Tube 2—5 drops of alcohol
   Tube 3—5 drops of bile solution
   Tube 4—5 drops of lemon juice
   Tube 5—10 drops of liquid detergent

5. Stopper each test tube and shake it vigorously five times.

6. Replace the tubes in the test-tube rack and allow them to remain undisturbed for 10 min. After 10 min, examine each tube. If a mixture is cloudy, some of the fat has broken down and mixed with the water.

7. To determine which mixtures appear cloudy or clear, hold each test tube in front of a sheet of newspaper. You can make your decision based on how distinctly you can see the newspaper through each solution. To determine relative cloudiness, compare each tube to Tube 1 by holding each tube against the newspaper background at the same time. Record your results in Table 1 as clear, very cloudy, slightly cloudy.

8. Some oil will remain on top of the water in each test tube. Determine whether the line that forms between oil and water is sharp or fuzzy. Record your answers in the table.

Laboratory Activity 2 (continued)

Data and Observations

1. What is the appearance of the oil and water in each test tube before you add anything else?

   _____

2. Record your observations of each mixture in Table 1.

Table 1

	Appearance of mixture	Appearance of line
Tube 1 (water, oil)		
Tube 2 (water, oil, alcohol)		
Tube 3 (water, oil, bile)		
Tube 4 (water, oil, lemon)		
Tube 5 (water, oil, detergent)		

Questions and Conclusions

1. Does water mix with fats (oils)?

   _____

   How can you tell?

   _____

2. Using the information in the table, how can you tell if fats (oils) are broken down so that they mix with water?

   _____

   _____

3. How can you tell if fats (oils) are not broken down and therefore do not mix with water?

   _____

4. Which chemicals caused the oil to break down the most?

   _____

5. Which chemicals caused a fuzzy line of separation between the oil and water?

   _____

6. Which chemical(s) used (alcohol, bile, lemon, detergent) is (are) not produced by the human digestive system?

Laboratory Activity 2 (continued)

7. a. Which chemical(s) is (are) produced by the human digestive system?

_____

_____

b. What is the function of those chemicals in our digestive system?

_____

_____

c. Did these chemicals perform in a similar way when used in a test tube containing fat (oil)?

_____

Explain.

_____

_____

8. What caused the mixing of oil and water in Tube 3?

_____

9. Is oil more dense than water? _____ How do you know?

_____

10. Why is detergent useful for washing grease from dishes?

_____

_____

11. If bile were not part of the digestive system, which of the following foods could not be properly digested? Underline the correct answers.

salad	bread	cake
salad dressing	butter	hamburger
bacon	milk	cola

Strategy Check

_____ Can you determine if fats mix with water?

_____ Can you list those chemicals that help to mix fats with water?

_____ Can you determine what substances best break down fats (oils)?

_____ Do any chemicals that help mix fats appear as part of your digestive system?

Analyzing Bones

Chapter 17

The skeletal system provides support for the body and protection for internal organs. In order to provide these functions, bones must be hard and strong. Scientists have discovered that the element calcium is responsible for making bones strong. Adding calcium to a bone can make it stronger, while removing calcium will make the bone weak and brittle. The amount of calcium in bones can change over time. Certain types of hard physical exercise and work can result in a gain of calcium to bones, while certain diseases and diets can result in a loss of calcium from bones.

Strategy

You will test the hardness of chicken bones before and after soaking them in different liquids. You will hypothesize which solutions will remove calcium from bones and test your hypothesis.

Materials

hydrogen peroxide
water
vinegar
a liquid chosen by the student
4 beakers or jars
chicken leg bones (boiled and cleaned)
forceps

CAUTION: *Wear gloves throughout this experiment. Do not taste, eat, or drink any materials used in the lab. Inform your teacher if you come into contact with any chemicals.*

Procedure

1. Four liquids will be tested for their effects on bones. Three of these liquids are listed in Table 1. You should choose a fourth liquid to test (lemon juice, fruit juices, soft drinks, milk, and so forth). Have your choice approved by your teacher and then record the type of liquid in Table 1 in Data and Observations.

2. Make a hypothesis about the effects each liquid will have on the strength of chicken bones. Write your hypothesis in Table 1.

3. Check the hardness of a chicken bone by gently twisting and bending the bone. Be careful not to crack or break the bone. Write your observations on the lines provided in the Data and Observations section.

4. Fill each beaker with one of the liquids. Label the beakers with your name and the kind of liquid.

5. Place a bone in each beaker of liquid. After 10 min, observe the bones and record in Table 2 any changes that you see.

6. After 48–72 h, use forceps to remove the bones from the liquids. Rinse the bones with water and observe them carefully. Record your observations in Table 2.

7. Retest the bones for hardness by twisting and bending. Record the results of the test in the Results column of Table 1.

Laboratory Activity 1 (continued)

Data and Observations

Table 1

Liquid	Hypothesis	Results
Water		
Vinegar		
Hydrogen peroxide		

Original Observations of bone hardness:

Table 2

Liquid	Observations (after 10 min)	Observations (after 48–72 h)
Water		
Vinegar		
Hydrogen peroxide		

Questions and Conclusions

1. What liquids removed calcium from bone?

_____

_____

_____

_____

Laboratory Activity 1 (continued)

2. How accurate were your hypotheses for the effects of each liquid?

_____

_____

_____

3. A baby's bones are softer than a teenager's. What might be a reason for this?

_____

_____

_____

_____

4. Some older persons suffer from a disease called osteoporosis, which results from calcium loss in bones. The bones weaken and are more likely to break. One way to help prevent osteoporosis is to eat calcium-rich foods. What foods could you eat to obtain more calcium?

_____

_____

_____

_____

5. Scientists have discovered that astronauts lose bone calcium while they are exposed to the microgravity of space. What might be a reason for this and what could astronauts do to prevent or slow the loss of calcium?

_____

_____

_____

_____

Strategy Check

_____ Can you test the hardness of chicken bones before and after soaking them in different liquids?

_____ Can you hypothesize which solutions will remove calcium from bones and test your hypothesis?

Muscle Action

Muscles attached to your eyelid allow you to blink your eyes. Is it necessary to remind yourself to blink or does the muscle do its job automatically? Can you stop yourself from blinking if you think about it? Muscles that do not have to be reminded are called involuntary. Those muscles that you control are called voluntary muscles. Do the eyelid muscles ever behave as both voluntary and involuntary muscles? Do some experimenting to see if you can answer this and a few other questions about blinking.

Strategy

You will perform three different experiments to discover if blinking is voluntary, involuntary, or both.

You will record your observations during these experiments so that you can make conclusions about blinking.

You will determine if blinking has any protective or useful purpose.

Materials

clock or watch with second hand
clear plastic sheet 30 × 30 cm
large cotton ball (about the size of a tennis ball)

Procedure

Part A

1. Look at your partner's eyes. Count the number of blinks in 1 min. NOTE: Do not try to reduce the number of normal blinks.
2. Record the number in Table 1 in Data and Observations.
3. Repeat steps 1 and 2 three more times.
4. Complete the table by determining the total and average number of blinks.
5. Repeat steps 1–4 with your partner looking at your eyes.

Part B

1. Watch your partner's eyes again. Time in *seconds* how long he/she can go without blinking. Record the number in Table 2 in Data and Observations.
2. Change roles again. Have your partner time in *seconds* how long you can go without blinking. Notice and remember the feeling of your eyes during this time.

Part C

1. Have your partner hold a sheet of clear plastic in front of his/her face.

NOTE: *The plastic sheet should not touch your partner's face.* As you throw a piece of cotton about the size of a tennis ball at the plastic, notice and record if your partner does or does not blink. Use a check mark to record this information in Table 3.

2. Repeat step 1 of Part C five more times and record the results each time.

Laboratory Activity 2 (continued)

Data and Observations

Table 1

Number of Blinks in 1 Minute		
Trial	Classmate	Yourself
1		
2		
3		
4		
Total		
Average		

Table 2

	Time without blinking (s)
You	
Your partner	

Table 3

Trial	Did blink	Did not blink
1		
2		
3		
4		
5		
6		

Laboratory Activity 2 (continued)

Questions and Conclusions

1. Does Part A show that blinking is voluntary or involuntary? Explain.

_____

_____

_____

2. Does Part A show that blinking is protective? Explain.

_____

_____

3. Does part B (no blinking) show voluntary or involuntary muscle action? Explain.

_____

_____

_____

4. It is important for people's eyes to remain moist. Describe how your eyes felt after not blinking. Do you think that blinking is helpful and protective? Explain.

_____

_____

_____

_____

5. How might you explain the fact that your average time and that of your partner in Part B are not the same?

_____

_____

_____

6. What does the activity with the cotton ball and plastic help prove? Explain.

_____

_____

_____

_____

Laboratory Activity 2 (continued)

7. What might happen if you were unable to blink?

_____

_____

_____

_____

Strategy Check

_____ Can you determine if blinking is voluntary, involuntary, or both?

_____ Can you use your observations to draw conclusions about blinking?

_____ Can you give evidence from your observations that blinking is protective or helpful?

Which brain side is dominant? Chapter 18

The human brain is divided into a left and a right side. Many things you do with the right side of your body are controlled by your brain's left side. Many things you do with the left side of your body are controlled by your brain's right side. If much of what you do is done by your body's right side, your dominant brain side is the left side. If much of what you do is done by your body's left side, your dominant brain side is the right side.

Strategy

You will check to see how many activities you do using your left hand or your right hand.
You will check to see how many activities you do using your left foot or your right foot.
You will find out whether you draw or see objects more to the right side or the left side.
You will find out whether the left side or the right side of your brain is dominant.

Materials

paper
red pencil

Procedure

1. Place a check mark in the proper column in Table 1 to show which hand you usually use to do the following tasks. Note: If you use either hand just as often, then check both columns.
   Tell which hand you use to:
   a. write your name
   b. wave "hello"
   c. bat while playing baseball
   d. place on top when folding your hands
   e. hold your spoon or fork while eating

2. Place a check mark in the proper column in Table 1 to show which foot you usually use to do the following tasks. Note: If you use either foot just as often, check both columns.
   Tell which foot you use to:
   a. start down a flight of stairs
   b. start up a flight of stairs
   c. catch yourself from falling as you lean forward

   d. start skipping
   e. place most weight on when you are standing
   f. start to run
   g. kick a ball

3. Draw, in the space provided, a simple side view of a dog. Place a check mark in the column in Table 1 that shows the direction the nose faces.

4. Draw a circle in the space provided with your *right* hand. Note the direction in which you made this circle. Now draw a circle with your *left* hand. Note the direction in which you made this circle. If both circles were drawn clockwise, mark the right column in Table 1. If both circles were drawn counterclockwise, mark the left column in Table 1. If you drew one circle in each direction, check both columns.

Laboratory Activity 1 (continued)

5. Roll a sheet of paper into a tube. Look through the tube at some distant object with both eyes open as shown in Figure 1. Then while looking through the tube at that distant object, close one eye and then the other. The eye that sees the object through the tube is your dominant eye. Place a check mark in the proper column in Table 1.

6. Total up the check marks for each column of Table 1 and place the total at the bottom of the columns.

Figure 1 – Finding Your Dominant Side

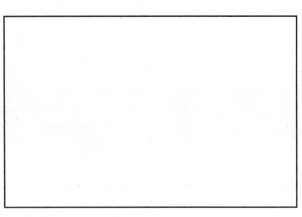

Dog drawing

Left hand

Right hand

Laboratory Activity 1 (continued)

Data and Observations

Volume Data		
Task	Left side	Right side
Write name		
Wave "hello"		
Bat		
Fold hands		
Hold spoon		
Walk down stairs		
Walk up stairs		
Catch from falling		
Skip		
Stand		
Start to run		
Take off shoe		
Leg on top		
Kick		
Dog drawing		
Circle drawing		
Dominant eye		
Totals =		

Questions and Conclusions

1. Which column in Table 1 has the most check marks? _____

2. Which column in Table 1 has the fewest check marks? _____

3. Which body side seems to be your dominant side? _____

4. The human cerebrum is divided into left and right sides.

   a. Which brain side controls the left side of your body? _____

   b. Which brain side controls the right side of your body? _____

5. The brain side that you use the most is said to be your dominant brain side. Which is your dominant brain side? (HINT: The answer will be the opposite from your answer to question 3.)

   _____

Laboratory Activity 1 (continued)

6. Look at Figure 2. It shows a top view of the brain. Label the following parts: *Left cerebrum side, right cerebrum side.* Use a red pencil to shade in your dominant brain side.

Figure 2

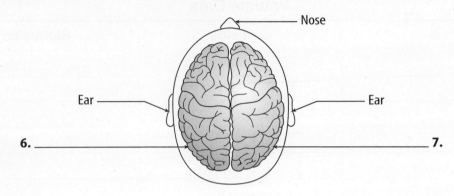

6. _____   7. _____

8. Your teacher will ask for a class survey of certain results. Complete the following data for your class.
   a. number of students who are right-handed and show the right body side as dominant

   _____

   b. number of students who are right-handed and show the left body side as dominant

   _____

   c. number of students who are left-handed and show the right body side as dominant

   _____

   d. number of students who are left-handed and show the left body side as dominant

   _____

9. Use your results from question number 9 to answer these questions:
   a. Does a person who uses his or her right hand for writing always show a dominant right

   body side? _____

   b. Does a person who uses his or her left hand for writing always show a dominant left

   body side? _____

Strategy Check

_____ Can you determine whether you use your left or right hand more?

_____ Can you determine whether you use your left or right foot more?

_____ Can you determine whether you draw or see objects more to the left or right side?

_____ Can you determine whether the left side or the right side of your brain is dominant?

Parts of the Eye

Chapter 18

Your eye is one of the most complex organs of your body. Much could be learned about eye functions if you could look inside a human eye and study its parts. This is not very practical, but you can study a cow eye. Cow eyes are very much like human eyes. Cow eyes have another advantage—they are bigger than human eyes.

Strategy

You will dissect a preserved cow eye.
You will identify the most important parts of the eye.
You will describe the functions of these eye parts.

Materials

cow eye (preserved)
dissecting pan
scalpel

Procedure

1. Cut away all of the muscle and fat that surround the rear ball part of the eyeball. Use a scalpel to start cutting the muscle and fat from the front toward the back of the eye. Remove only small portions of tissue at a time. **CAUTION:** *Use care when cutting to avoid injury.* Do not remove the optic nerve as you trim the eyeball of fat and muscle. (The optic nerve can be seen as a white, round, pencil-thick bundle of nerves surrounded by a dark-colored layer of muscle tissue at the back of the eye.) Use the dash line shown in Figure 1 as a guide to how much muscle and fat must be removed.

Figure 1

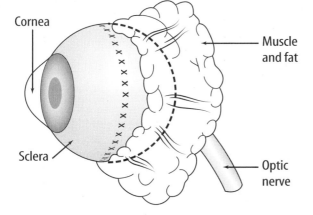

2. You are now ready to cut into the eye. Cut in a circular pattern into the eye at the position marked in Figure 1 with X marks. You must cut through a tough outer layer called the sclera.

3. Cut the eye in half, separating the front from the back. A jellylike material will probably fall out as the eye is cut in half. This is the vitreous humor, a transparent jelly that fills the inside of the eye. The lens is a marble-shaped structure that may also fall out of the eye.

4. Place the front portion of the eye with the outside facing down. Use Figure 2b to help you identify the ciliary muscles, iris, pupil, and cornea. Hold the front portion of the eye up to the light and observe the cornea. The cornea will not be completely transparent, but it is transparent in a living eye.

5. Place the back portion of the eye with the inside facing up. Examine the back portion of the eye Figure 2a. You should have the cut surface facing up. You should notice a thin, wrinkled, whitish tissue on the inside along the back. This is the retina. The retina in a living eye is smooth. NOTE: The retina can be removed for closer examination. Observe that it attaches to the back of the eye. This is the blind spot leading to the optic nerve.

Laboratory Activity 2 (continued)

6. At the back of the eyeball is a bluish layer called the tapetum. This layer acts as a reflective surface and is found only in certain animals. Push the tapetum aside at its cut edge to find the choroid layer directly below.

7. Examine the solid, round, yellowish structure (Figure 2c) that fell out when you opened the eyeball. This is the lens. It is covered with a layer of fine muscle fibers that control the shape of the lens. Hold it up to the light. The lens does not appear completely transparent now, but it is transparent in a living eye. **CAUTION:** *Wash your hands thoroughly after handling the eye.*

8. Correctly label Figure 3 in Data and Observations, which shows the side view diagram of the eye.

9. Record the parts of the eye you identified and their functions in Table 1. You may use reference books and your textbook to complete the table.

Figure 2

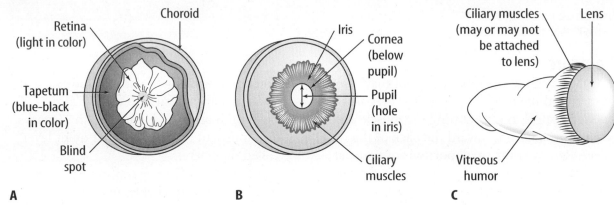

Retina (light in color) — Choroid — Iris — Cornea (below pupil) — Ciliary muscles (may or may not be attached to lens) — Lens

Tapetum (blue-black in color) — Pupil (hole in iris)

Blind spot — Ciliary muscles — Vitreous humor

A   **B**   **C**

Data and Observations

Figure 3

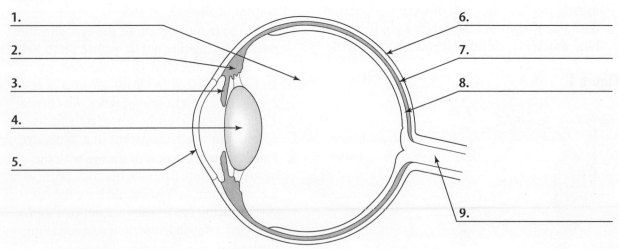

1.
2.
3.
4.
5.
6.
7.
8.
9.

Name _____ Date _____ Class _____

Laboratory Activity 2 (continued)

Table 1

Structure of the Eye	
Part	**Function**
10.	
11.	
12.	
13.	
14.	
15.	
16.	
17.	
18.	
19.	

Questions and Conclusions

1. Give a possible difference between what you observed in a preserved eye compared with a living eye for the following parts:

   a. retina _____

   b. lens _____

   c. cornea _____

   d. vitreous humor _____

Copyright © Glencoe/McGraw-Hill, a division of the McGraw-Hill Companies, Inc.

Laboratory Activity 2 (continued)

2. List the following eye parts in the order that light passes through them: vitreous humor, retina, lens, cornea, pupil.

_____

_____

3. Explain why it is important that the lens and cornea be transparent in a living eye.

_____

_____

_____

_____

Strategy Check

_____ Can you dissect a preserved cow eye?

_____ Can you identify the most important parts of the eye?

_____ Can you describe the function of each part you examined?

The Effects of Epinephrine on a Planarian

Hormones are small molecules released in tiny amounts to affect target tissues. Their effects on an organism are easily observed. For instance, epinephrine is a hormone that increases heart rate and metabolic rate. In humans, epinephrine prepares the body physiologically for stress. In other animals, epinephrine prepares the system for flight or escape.

Strategy

You will observe and record the behavior of a planarian with and without a 0.01 percent solution of epinephrine.

Materials

pond water
petri dish
one piece of 1/4 in graph paper
planarian
medicine dropper
0.01 percent epinephrine solution

Procedure

1. Put enough pond water in the petri dish to just cover the bottom.
2. Place the petri dish on top of the sheet of graph paper so that the squares show through the bottom.
3. Carefully transfer one planarian to the center of the dish. Wait five minutes while the planarian adjusts to its surroundings.
4. Now begin recording the planarian's behavior. Every minute for five minutes, count the number of different boxes the planarian touches. Record the number in the data table in the Data and Observations section.

5. Use the medicine dropper to place five drops of 0.01 percent epinephrine solution to the petri dish. Wait one minute.
6. Now record the effect of epinephrine on the planarian's behavior. Follow the procedures in step 4. Record your observations in the data table in the Data and Observations section.
7. Repeat steps 5 and 6 two times. In all, you will then have observations for 5, 10, and 15 drops of epinephrine solution.

Laboratory Activity 1 (continued)

Data and Observations

		Number of Squares Crossed by Planarian		
Time	No epinephrine	5 Drops epinephrine	10 Drops epinephrine	15 Drops epinephrine
1. First minute				
2. Second minute				
3. Third minute				
4. Fourth minute				
5. Fifth minute				

Questions and Conclusions

1. Describe the planarian's behavior when it was first placed in the Petri dish.

_____

_____

_____

_____

2. What happened when the first 5 drops of epinephrine solution were added? The second 5 drops? The third 5 drops?

_____

_____

_____

_____

3. Other than a change in the number of squares crossed, describe any other changes in the behavior of your planarian after the epinephrine was added.

_____

_____

_____

_____

Laboratory Activity 1 (continued)

4. Epinephrine is a hormone that prepares an animal for flight or escape. Did your observations support this? If not, suggest possible explanations.

_____

_____

_____

_____

5. How could the results of this activity be made more accurate?

_____

_____

_____

Strategy Check

_____ Can you observe and record the behavior of a planarian with and without a 0.01 percent solution of epinephrine?

Fetal Development

Chapter 19

A human body usually develops inside its mother for 38 weeks. During the first eight weeks it is called an embryo. From the ninth to the thirty-eighth week it is called a fetus. Different organs and systems develop at different times during these 38 weeks. The age of a developing baby can be determined by its length.

Strategy
You will measure the length of five diagrams of a human fetus.
You will match events taking place during development with the proper age of the fetus.

Materials
ruler (metric)

Procedure
1. Measure the length of each fetus from crown to rump. Record in Table 3.
2. To determine actual length, multiply each measurement by 2.75. Record in Table 3.
3. Record the events occurring to each fetus in Table 2. Events are listed in Table 1.

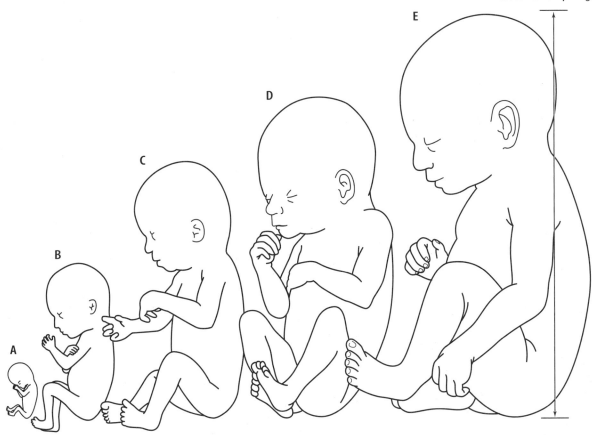

Crown to rump length

Questions and Conclusions
1. Explain the changes that take place in a fetus between week 9 and week 38.

   a. body hair _____

   b. the eyes _____

   c. sex determination _____

~~Lab~~oratory Activity 2 (continued)

2. A fetus born with a crown to rump length of 270 mm will have a difficult time of survival. About how old is a fetus of this length? _____

3. It is possible to "see" a fetus using ultrasound equipment. How might ultrasounds taken at 9 and 20 weeks of age differ? _____

Strategy Check

_____ Can you measure the crown to rump length of five diagrams of a human fetus?

_____ Can you match events during development with specific ages of a fetus?

Data and Observations

Table 1

Event	Length	Event	Length
24 weeks old	230 mm	eyes open	300 mm
sex can be determined	140 mm	32 weeks old	300 mm
eyes closed	50 mm	mother feels movement	140 mm
all organs well developed	230 mm	body "chubby" looking	300 mm
9 weeks old	50 mm	body hair is gone	360 mm
16 weeks old	140 mm	can grasp with hand	360 mm
body covered with hair	230 mm	sex cannot be determined	50 mm
38 weeks old	360 mm		

Table 2

A	B	C	D	E

Table 3

Fetus	Length in (mm)	× 2.75	Actual length
A		× 2.75	
B		× 2.75	
C		× 2.75	
D		× 2.75	
E		× 2.75	

Communities

The human population of an area is made up of all the people who live there. The community in which people live includes other populations as well, populations that might include squirrels, honey bees, and maple trees. All the populations living together in a certain area make up a community. The producers in a community make the energy-rich molecules that can be used as food. The consumers obtain food by eating other organisms, either living or dead, that contain the energy-rich molecules. All the organisms in a community interact with each other.

Strategy

You will study a community.
You will identify organisms in the community that are producers or consumers.

Materials

thermometer
paper
pencil

Procedure

Part A

1. In Table 1 in the Data and Observations section, list four living things commonly found in each type of community shown below. For example, a farm community might have humans, cows, horses, chickens, wheat, corn, and soybeans.

2. Classify the living things listed in Table 1 as producers or consumers. Producers can make their own food and are usually green. Consumers cannot make their own food and usually are not green. Circle the producers and underline the consumers.

Laboratory Activity 1 (continued)

Part B

1. With your teacher's help, choose a nearby community to study.
2. Record in Table 2 the common names of the consumers and producers that you observed in your selected community. Note the approximate number of each type of organism. Continue your list on a separate sheet of paper, if needed.
3. Moisture, light, season of the year, and temperature can influence communities. Observe these conditions in the community you are studying. Then record your observations below in the Data and Observations section.

Data and Observations

Table 1

Type of community	Names of organisms
Farm	
Forest	
Desert	
Ocean	

Table 2

Producers		Consumers	
Type	Number	Type	Number
Example: Grass		Example: Mice	

1. Location: _____

2. Date of observation: _____

3. Amount of direct sunlight: _____

4. Evidence of moisture: _____

5. Air temperature: _____

Laboratory Activity 1 (continued)

Questions and Conclusions

1. Define community.

   _____

2. What is a producer?

   _____

3. What is a consumer?

   _____

4. Do all communities have both consumers and producers? Explain.

   _____

   _____

5. How many kinds of producers did you find in the community you studied?

   _____

   _____

6. How many kinds of consumers did you find?

   _____

   _____

7. Did you find more producers than consumers? Explain why there would be more of one than the other.

   _____

   _____

8. What do producers provide consumers?

   _____

   _____

Strategy Check

_____ Can you study a community?

_____ Can you identify the producers and consumers in the community?

Changes in Predator and Prey Populations

A predator is an animal that kills and eats another animal. A fox is an example of a predator. The prey is the animal killed by a predator. A rabbit is an example of an animal that is prey for the fox.

The sizes of the predator and prey populations can change with time. Biologists sometimes need to know the sizes of certain predator and prey populations. They can sample the population by trapping and/or counting the animals. The result of the samplings changes as the populations change.

Strategy

You will set up a model of predator and prey populations and observe changes in the results you get from sampling as the populations change.

You will construct a graph showing your results.

Materials

101 brown beans
17 white beans
small paper bag
colored pencils

Procedure

Part A—Sampling a Population

1. Read this report about animals on the abandoned Linworth farm.

   The Linworth farm was abandoned in 1990, when an interstate highway was built through it. In April 1997, two biologists decided to study how the fox and rabbit populations on the 40 hectares of farmland were changing. The scientists counted rabbits by trapping and releasing them and counted foxes with binoculars. The biologists trapped and released 23 rabbits; they saw 2 foxes. The scientist continued their observations in the spring and fall for several years.

2. Put 92 brown beans and 8 white beans into a bag. The brown beans represent rabbits, and the white beans represent foxes. Note that these numbers are four times the observed number of animals in the example above. The observed animals are the sample. The larger numbers represent the numbers of rabbits and foxes in the actual populations.

3. Shake the bag with the beans. Select a bean without looking. Record your results in Table 1 in the Data and Observations section. If you picked a brown bean, put a mark under "observed" in the rabbit column. If you picked a white bean, put a mark in the fox column.

4. Return the bean to the bag. Select another bean, record the result in Table 1 and return the bean to the bag. Repeat this procedure until you have results recorded for 25 beans, which is 25 percent of the actual numbers in the populations.

5. Add together the numbers of brown beans selected. Record the number in Table 1. Repeat for the white beans.

Part B—Recording Changes in Populations

1. Examine Table 2, which explains how to change numbers of beans to show how the rabbit and fox populations changed as a result of changes in environmental factors.

Laboratory Activity 2 (continued)

2. Use the information in Table 2 and the method described in Part A to sample the populations of rabbits and foxes nine more times. Enter your data in Table 3.
   a. Start with the information for the first date in Table 2, October 1997. Add and remove beans as directed to represent the changes described.
   b. Select 25 more beans, returning them to the bag each time. Make marks in the appropriate columns in Table 3, and fill in the total number of brown beans and white beans selected.

c. Repeat this procedure for every date in Table 3. When you come to a date in Table 3 that is not included in Table 2, assume there was no change in the populations. However, conduct a new sampling even though the total populations were unchanged.

3. Fill in the graph on the next page using the data from the population samplings that you recorded in Table 3. Use two different colored columns for each date, one for rabbits and one for foxes.

Data and Observations

Table 1

Sampling Data				
Date	Rabbits (brown beans)		Foxes (white beans)	
	Observed	Total	Observed	Total
April 1997				

Table 2

Changes in Population		
Sampling date	Rabbit population	Fox population
October 1997	The winter was harsh, and food was inadequate. Many rabbits died. Remove 10 brown beans.	Foxes ate pheasants as well as rabbits. Fox numbers increased. Add 2 white beans.
October 1998	Food was plentiful. Rabbits moved into the area. Add 15 brown beans.	Foxes had larger litters than usual. Add 2 white beans.
April 1999	Disease killed many rabbits. Remove 8 brown beans.	Food supply was low due to disease among the rabbits. Some foxes left the area. Remove 3 white beans.
October 1999	Spring came early. Rabbits could breed earlier. Add 12 brown beans.	Food was plentiful. Foxes moved into the area. Add 8 white beans.
April 2000	No change in population.	Inadequate food to feed the increased fox population. Some foxes moved out. Remove 4 white beans.
October 2000	The farm was opened to hunters, who killed pheasants. Foxes ate more rabbits. Remove 14 brown beans.	Hunters shot some foxes. Remove 2 white beans.

Laboratory Activity 2 (continued)

Table 3

Date	Rabbits (brown beans)		Foxes (white beans)	
	Observed	Total	Observed	Total
October 1997				
April 1998				
October 1998				
April 1999				
October 1999				
April 2000				
October 2000				
April 2001				
October 2001				

Figure 1

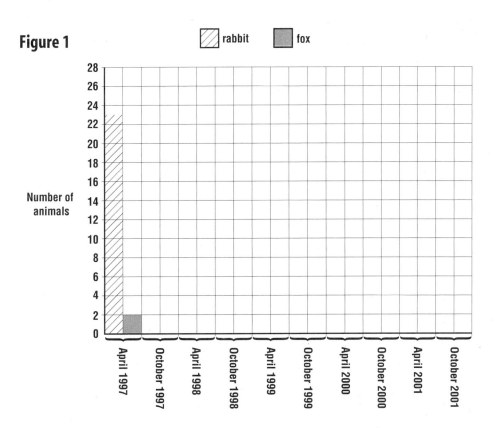

Laboratory Activity 2 (continued)

Questions and Conclusions

1. In this example, which animal is the predator and which is the prey?

_____

2. How did the data from your sampling in Part A compare with those of the two biologists in April 1997?

_____

3. Give two factors that caused a decrease in the rabbit population.

_____

4. Give two factors that caused an increase in the rabbit population.

_____

_____

5. Give three factors that caused a decrease in the fox population.

_____

_____

6. Give three factors that caused an increase in the fox population.

_____

_____

7. What happened to the rabbits when the pheasant population decreased?

_____

_____

Strategy Check

_____ Can you set up a model of predator and prey populations and observe changes as populations change?

_____ Can you construct a graph showing your results?

LAB 1 Laboratory Activity

Succession Communities and Grasses

Chapter 21

Once lichens and other pioneer species die and organic matter is added to the soil, other plants are able to grow. Grasses are a characteristic species of primary and secondary succession. They are tough and adaptable, grow quickly and readily, and further enrich the soil when they die.

Strategy

You will observe the effect of sunlight and water on the growth of grass.

You will identify differences between the characteristics of a succession community and the characteristics of a climax community.

Materials

four small plastic pots filled with soil and planted with grass seed
permanent marker
small box open only at one end
water

Procedure

1. Label the pots 1, 2, 3, and 4.
2. Place pot 1 in a location that will receive a lot of indirect sunlight.
3. Cover pot 2 with the box. Place it next to pot 1.
4. Water pots 1 and 2 with the same amount of water twice a week. Keep the soil moist but not wet.
5. Place pots 3 and 4 in the same location as plants 1 and 2.
6. Water pot 3 daily. Keep the soil wet.

7. Do not water pot 4.
8. In the Data and Observations table, write a hypothesis describing how you think the amount of light will affect pots 1 and 2. Write another hypothesis describing how you think the amount of water will affect pots 1, 3, and 4.
9. Care for the plants daily for three weeks. Record observations at the end of each week.

Data and Observations

Hypothesis			
Plants 1 and 2 (light)			
Plants 1, 3 and 4 (water)			
Observations			
Plant	**Week 1**	**Week 2**	**Week 3**
1			
2			
3			
4			

Laboratory Activity 1 (continued)

Questions and Conclusions

1. What was the effect of the amount of light on pots 1 and 2? How does your hypothesis differ from the results?

_____

_____

_____

_____

_____

2. What was the effect of the amount of water on pots 1, 3, and 4? How does your hypothesis differ from the results?

_____

_____

_____

3. What characteristics of grass do you think make it well-suited as a late primary or secondary succession plant?

_____

_____

_____

4. Would you find grasses in a climax community? Why or why not?

_____

_____

_____

_____

_____

_____

Strategy Check

_____ Can you observe the effect of sunlight and water on the growth of grass?

_____ Can you identify differences between the characteristics of succession and climax communities?

Exploring Life in Pond Water

Chapter 21

Looking through a microscope, you can see a miniature world of many, many microorganisms. In a single drop of pond water, you might be able to see protists, bacteria, plants, and tiny animals. Because the ecosystem of a pond is not uniform throughout, different organisms live in different parts of the pond. Water collected from the surface and from near the sediment will contain some of the same organisms, but there will be some organisms that live in only one area or the other.

Strategy
You will examine two samples of pond water under the microscope.
You will identify some of the organisms that exist in each sample of pond water.
You will compare the organisms found near the surface to those found near the bottom of the pond.

Materials
water collected from the surface of a pond
dropper
microscope slides (2)
coverslips (2)
microscope
water collected near the bottom of a pond

Procedure
1. Use the dropper to place one drop of surface pond water on a clean microscope slide. Carefully put the coverslip on the drop.
2. Examine the surface pond water under low and high power magnification of the microscope. Carefully move the slide so that you are able to examine all areas of the slide.
3. Use the drawings in the Data and Observations section to identify the organisms you observe. On the lines under the drawings, indicate which organisms were observed in the surface pond water.

4. Repeat steps 1 through 3 for a drop of water from the bottom of the pond.
5. Complete Table 1 in the Data and Observations section by entering the microorganisms that you observe in the water from the surface and the bottom of the pond.
6. Enter your data in the table your teacher has prepared on the board by putting a mark by each organism that you observed in your samples. When all students have entered their data, complete Table 2 by summarizing the data from the table on the board.

Laboratory Activity 2 (continued)

Data and Observations

1. *Oscillatoria*

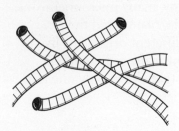

_____

2. *Paramecium*

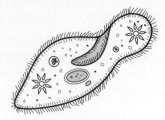

_____

3. *Vorticella*

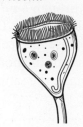

_____

4. *Daphnia* (waterflea)

_____

5. *Euglena*

_____

6. *Amoeba*

_____

7. Rotifers

_____

8. Nematodes

_____

9. *Cyclops*

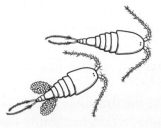

_____

10. Diatoms

_____

11. *Volvox*

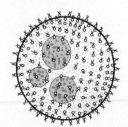

_____

12. Desmids

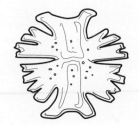

_____

Laboratory Activity 2 (continued)

Table 1

Individual Data	
Organisms found in surface pond water	**Organisms found near pond bottom**

Table 2

Group Data		
Organism	**Near surface**	**Near bottom**
Oscillatoria		
Paramecium		
Vorticella		
Daphnia		
Euglena		
Amoeba		
Rotifers		
Nematodes		
Cyclops		
Diatoms		
Volvox		
Desmids		

Laboratory Activity 2 (continued)

Questions and Conclusions

1. Did you find different organisms in the surface and deep pond water samples? Explain.

_____

_____

2. What factors might influence why some organisms are found only in surface pond water or only in deep pond water?

_____

_____

3. Because a pond is an ecosystem that changes all the time, experimental variables might have an impact on your observations. Explain how each of the following might influence the organisms observed:

   a. season of the year

   _____

   b. delay between when the sample was collected and the experiment was performed

   _____

   c. depth of collection site for water from the bottom of the pond

   _____

   d. distance from shore that the surface water was collected

   _____

4. In what ways might human activity impact the pond water ecosystem?

_____

_____

_____

Strategy Check

_____ Can you examine samples of pond water under the microscope?

_____ Can you identify the organisms that exist in each sample of pond water?

_____ Can you compare the organisms found on the surface of a pond to those found near the bottom?

Water Pollution

Polluting substances are added to the environment in many ways. Detergents, fertilizers, and garbage often wash into streams. These substances can influence the growth of algae in freshwater. Algae add oxygen to water. Problems arise when the algae die and decompose. Decomposition of algae by bacteria uses oxygen resulting in a net oxygen loss from the water. Therefore, other organisms that need oxygen to survive begin to die off.

Strategy

You will test the effects of detergent, fertilizer, and garbage on the growth of algae in water. You will observe and record changes that occur in water environments.

Materials

labels
4 glass jars (1-L, with lids)
aged tap water
water containing algae
graduated cylinder
detergent
fertilizer (liquid)
plant peelings (potato, apple, orange)

Procedure

1. Label the jars, 1, 2, 3, and 4. Half fill each jar with aged tap water. Add water containing algae until each jar is 3/4 full. **CAUTION:** *Always wash your hands after handling microbes.*
2. Add 5 mL of detergent to jar 1.
3. Add 5 mL of fertilizer to jar 2.
4. Add some plant peelings to jar 3.

5. Do not add anything to jar 4. It will be the control.
6. Put the lid on each of the jars.
7. Place the jars in the light: on a windowsill or underneath a light source.
8. Observe the jars every other day for two weeks. Compare jars 1, 2, and 3 with jar 4. Record your observations in Tables 1–4.

Data and Observations

Table 1

Jar 1, Detergent Added	
Date	Observations

Table 2

Jar 2, Fertilizer Added	
Date	Observations

Laboratory Activity 1 (continued)

Table 3

Jar 3, Peelings Added	
Date	Observations

Table 4

Jar 4, Nothing Added	
Date	Observations

Laboratory Activity 1 (continued)

Questions and Conclusions

1. **a.** Which jar(s) had the greatest algae growth?

_____

  b. What was added to this jar?

_____

2. **a.** Which jar(s) had the least algae growth?

_____

  b. What was added to this jar?

_____

3. What would happen to a lake if a large amount of fertilizer were dumped in it?

_____

_____

_____

4. What were the pollutants in this experiment?

_____

_____

5. What is water pollution?

_____

_____

Strategy Check

_____ Can you test the growth of algae when substances were added to water containing algae?

_____ Can you observe and record the changes in water containing algae and pollutants?

What to Do with Plastic

Landfills receive more and more plastics every day. Plastics do not decompose readily since there are no natural bacteria or processes that can break most of them down. Instead, one of the solutions for keeping the amount of plastic wastes low is recycling. There are many different kinds of plastics, and some are good for recycling into certain products while others are not. To help identify which plastics are best for recycling, the Society of the Plastics Industry (SPI) has created a special code system to let you know how to recycle the plastic. In this exercise you will find and identify the recycling codes for a variety of objects. You will also investigate what, if any, recycling plans your school or community has.

Strategy

You will identify the recycling codes on plastic materials.
You will describe your school's or community's recycling program.

Materials

You will need as many plastic objects with different recycling codes as possible for identification. The table of codes provides a guide to the different recycling symbols. Your teacher might ask if all students can bring a bag of a unused or cleaned waste plastic items from home.

Procedure

1. Go to the place in the room where the plastic items are collected. Pick one or two items and take them to your desk.
2. Find the recycling code and look for the number. Record the object in the second column of the correct row in Table 2. Describe what the object is.
3. In the third column of the data table describe what the characteristics of the object are. You can do this by finding the characteristics in Table 1 on the next page.
4. In the fourth column of the data table write the chemical name for the type of plastic you have. This information is also in the table at the beginning of the lab.
5. Continue this procedure until all of the items have been described. You will have many entries in each column space.

SPI code	Name	Features	Common uses
△ 1 PETE	Polyethylene Terephthalate	Tough; slick; shiny and transparent; sinks in water; slightly rigid; sickly sweet smell when burned	Soda, juice and mineral water bottles; clear detergent bottles; recording tape; etc.
△ 2 HDPE	High density polyethylene	Tough; Slightly waxy; matte finish; buoyant; relatively flexible; waxy scent when burned	Milk and water jugs; matte finish juice bottles; ethyl alcohol; shampoo and most detergent bottles
△ 3 V	Vinyl or polyvinyl chloride	Tough; smooth; shiny; sinks in water; slightly rigid; acrid scent when burned.	Salad dressing bottles; blister packs; some spring water bottles; some medicine bottles; etc.
△ 4 LDPE	Low density polyethylene	Tough; slightly waxy; shiny to matte; transparent to opaque; flexible and stretchable; floats in water; waxy scent when burned.	Plastic coatings; plastic bags; food containers and lids; etc.
△ 5 PP	Polypropylene	Hard; tough; smooth shiny or glossy; floats in water; chemical scent and taffy-like consistency when burned.	Inner bags of cereal boxes; combs; some junk food bags and wrappers; medicine containers; rope and strapping; etc.
△ 6 PS	Polystyrene	Slick and glossy unless foamed; smooth; easy to crack; scratch-resistant unless foamed; sinks unless foamed.	Plastic cutlery; vitamin bottles; carry-out containers; egg cartons; Styrofoam©; disposable plastic cups; some yogurt containers; etc.
△ 7 OTHER	All other resins; multi-layered plastics	Varies	Squeeze bottles; water cooler bottles; microwave trays; most junk food bags; etc.

Laboratory Activity 2 (continued)

Table 2

SPI code	Object	Features	Chemical name
1 PETE			
2 HDPE			
3 V			
4 LDPE			
5 PP			
6 PS			
7 OTHER			

Laboratory Activity 2 (continued)

Questions and Conclusions

1. Where on the containers did you find the SPI Code?

_____

2. Why do you think it is always in approximately the same place?

_____

_____

3. For which plastic code did you find the most specimens?

_____

4. For which plastic code did you find the fewest specimens?

_____

5. Why do you think there is a difference between the numbers of items under the separate codes?

_____

_____

6. Do you or your family members recycle plastics? Why or why not?

_____

_____

_____

7. Does your school have a recycling program? If so, what kinds of items are recycled?

_____

_____

8. Does your neighborhood or community have a recycling program? If so, what kinds of items are recycled?

_____

_____

9. Do you think we could all do a better job of recycling and using recycled products? Why or why not?

_____

_____

_____

Strategy Check

_____ Can you identify the recycling codes on plastic materials?

_____ Can you describe your school's or community's recycling program?

Chemical Weathering

Chapter 23

Rocks are mixtures of minerals that are either elements or chemical compounds. Chemical weathering is the chemical reaction of these minerals with carbon dioxide, water, oxygen, or other substances at Earth's surface. For example, in minerals containing iron, the iron reacts with oxygen in the air and moisture to form rust. Rotted plant material combines with water to form humic acids that cause chemical weathering.

Strategy

You will cause a chemical reaction between a copper strip and combined salt and vinegar at room temperature.

You will observe a chemical reaction between iron and atmospheric oxygen and moisture.

Materials

copper strip (dirty)
pie pan (disposable)
graduated cylinder
salt
vinegar (white)
iron (II) sulfate, $FeSO_4$
water
beaker

Procedure

1. For the first activity, place a copper strip in the pie pan and place 5 mL salt on the strip.
2. Carefully pour 30 mL of vinegar over the copper. Record your observations in Table 1.
3. Wash the salt and vinegar off the copper. **CAUTION:** *The material formed is an acid. Avoid contact with skin and clothing.*
4. For a separate activity, mix 5 g of iron (II) sulfate in 50 mL of water.

CAUTION: *Iron(II) sulfate is poisonous. Avoid contact with skin.* Record the color of the solution and any other observations in Table 1.

5. Let both the beaker and the copper stand undisturbed overnight.
6. Next day, observe the beaker and the copper. Record your observations in Table 1.

Data and Observations

Table 1

	Start	Next day
1. Copper strip		
2. Beaker $FeSO_4$		

Laboratory Activity 1 (continued)

Questions and Conclusions

1. What happened to the copper when you poured the vinegar over the salt?

   _____

   _____

2. Is cleaning copper a chemical or physical process? _____

3. Explain what happens to the clean copper left in the air overnight.

   _____

   _____

4. Why does this reaction follow the cleaning of the copper?

   _____

   _____

5. Explain what you observed in the beaker of $FeSO_4$.

   _____

   _____

6. Is this a physical or chemical change? _____

7. Explain the rust-colored stains you see on some rocks. _____

   _____

8. How might a soil layer protect rock from chemical weathering?

   _____

   _____

Strategy Check

_____ Can you cause a chemical reaction between a copper strip and combined salt and vinegar at room temperature?

_____ Can you observe a chemical reaction between iron and atmospheric oxygen and moisture?

Soil Infiltration by Groundwater

Chapter 23

Whether rainwater enters the soil or runs off the surface depends on many factors. One of the most important factors is the type of soil. Also, the rate at which rainwater enters the soil determines whether or not flooding occurs and whether or not septic tanks can be installed safely in a given region. If liquid from the tanks flows outward faster than the soil can absorb it, no filtering action occurs, and sewage reaches the surface and contaminates the area.

This laboratory activity is one of the tests that engineers use to decide if septic tanks are acceptable for a given area. Engineers make the test directly in the ground, sinking the can as far as possible. You may perform the test in the same way, or you may construct a simulated soil sequence and do your testing in the classroom.

Strategy

You will measure the rate at which water filters through soil.
You will plot the rate of infiltration against time.
You will compare various materials to see which are most suitable for filtering groundwater.

Materials

can opener
juice can (large)
cheesecloth (30 cm × 30 cm)
tape (masking)
dishpan or sink
2 pencils
beaker (500 mL)

gravel (500 mL)
slab clay
fine sand (500 mL)
soil (500 mL)
cardboard (thin)
scissors
plastic bucket

water
pointed stick (30 cm long)
pen (felt-tip)
watch with second hand
metric ruler
graph paper

Procedure

1. With the can opener, cut out both ends of the can. Place the cheesecloth across the bottom of the can and fasten it with tape.
2. Place the can in the dishpan, cloth side down. Raise the can slightly by resting it on the two pencils.
3. Do not fill the can more than half full. Place a layer of gravel in the bottom of the can. Place a layer of clay on the layer of gravel. Place a layer of sand on top of the clay. Place a thick layer of soil on top of the sand.
4. Make a cardboard cover for the can. Cut a small hole (about the diameter of the pointed stick) in the cardboard cover. Cut a small portion from one side of the cover.

Through this hole, you will be able to observe the water level.
5. Fill the rest of the can with water. Place the cover over the top of the can.
6. After about one minute, insert the pointed stick into the can through the small hole until it just touches the top of the water. With the felt-tip pen, draw a line on the stick where it intersects the side of the can.
7. Mark the water depth on the stick every 60 seconds until the soil appears above the water. Determine the various water depths by measuring from the point of the stick to the first mark, second mark, and so on. Record your data in Table 1.

Laboratory Activity 2 (continued)

Data and Observations

Table 1

Time (min)	Water depth (cm)	Time (min)	Water depth (cm)

Graph your data on a sheet of graph paper using the vertical axis for depth of water (cm) and the horizontal axis for time (min).

Questions and Conclusions

1. Is the rate of infiltration constant? Explain.

   _____

   _____

2. Would the rate of infiltration be faster in wet soil or dry soil? Why?

   _____

   _____

3. Which layer infiltrates most slowly? Explain how you got your answer.

   _____

   _____

4. Which layer is most likely to allow the water to move through it too rapidly to be a good filter? Explain how you could design an experiment to find out.

   _____

   _____

Strategy Check

_____ Can you measure the rate at which water filters through soil?

_____ Can you make a graph that shows the rate of infiltration?

_____ Can you compare various materials to see which is suitable for filtering groundwater?

Mass Movements

The force of gravity causes loose material to move down slope. Sometimes water helps to move the material. Water makes the material heavier and more slippery.

Down slope movements of earth materials may be sudden or slow. Landslides and mudflows are sudden movements. Rocky slopes tend to move as landslides; clay and sand materials may become mudflows.

Creep is an example of slow earth movement. Even when a slope is covered by vegetation, the soil may creep to a lower level.

Strategy

You will cause mass movements.
You will classify the mass movements.

Materials

stream table with hose
4 wood blocks
plastic bucket
protractor
1 L clay
1 L sand
sprinkling can
water
1 L gravel
meterstick

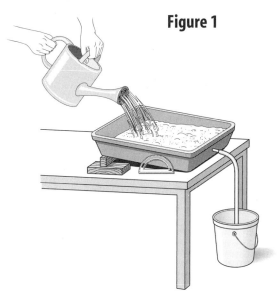

Figure 1

Procedure

1. Set up the stream table as shown in Figure 1.
2. Place the protractor with its flat edge down on the table that is supporting the stream table. Position the protractor next to the lower end of the stream table. Use the protractor to measure the slope angle of the stream table. Record the angle in Table 1.
3. Place the clay in the upper end of the stream table.
4. Pour the sand over the clay. Wet the sand and clay thoroughly until it moves.
5. Observe and record in Table 1 how the mass moves.

6. Add two more blocks under the stream table. Measure and record the new slope angle of the stream table.
7. Move the sand and clay back to the upper end of the stream table.
8. Pour water over the sand and clay until it moves. Record how the mass moves.
9. Remove the sand and clay. Spread a thin layer of clay in the upper end of the table.
10. Spread gravel over the clay. Pour water over the clay and gravel and observe the motion. Record your observations.

Laboratory Activity 1 (continued)

Data and Observations
Table 1

Material	Slope angle (°)	Speed of movement
Sand, clay		
Sand, clay		
Clay, gravel		

Questions and Conclusions

1. What type of mass movement did you cause in steps 3 and 4?

2. What type of mass movement did you cause in steps 7 and 8?

3. What caused the difference in speed between these two mass movements?

4. What type of mass movement did you cause in steps 9 and 10?

5. Which type of mass movement would occur during an extended period of heavy rain on a filled area? Explain.

6. Which type of mass movement, creep or mudflow, is most destructive? Explain.

7. In an area that receives abundant rainfall, how are steep slopes kept from moving downhill?

Strategy Check

_____ Can you cause mass movements?

_____ Can you classify mass movements?

Modeling a Glacier

Valley glaciers start in the mountains where snow collects and remains year after year. When the amount of snow accumulation exceeds the amount of snow melting and the snow mass is thick enough, gravity starts the glacier moving downslope. The glacier can take over a river valley as it moves toward a lower elevation. The glacier gouges and scrapes the surface beneath the ice and changes the landscape in many ways.

Strategy

You will construct a model of a valley glacier.
You will show the rugged features a valley glacier forms as it moves and melts.

Materials

cardboard base (21.5 cm × 28 cm)
4 colors of modeling clay
paper for labels
tape (clear)
toothpicks

Procedure

1. On the cardboard base, form a mountain from the darkest piece of clay.
2. Use white clay to show the position of a glacier on your mountain.
3. Show the erosional features of the glacier. Use the toothpicks and paper to make little flags.
4. You might wish to use a thin layer of green clay to show where vegetation has begun to appear.

5. Be sure to model each of the following features: U-shaped valley, cirque, terminal moraine, horn, and outwash plain.
6. Draw a diagram of your model under Data and Observations on the next page. Label the features.

Questions and Conclusions

Write a summary explaining how valley glaciers form and move and how they change the landscape.

_____

_____

_____

_____

_____

Laboratory Activity 2 (continued)

Data and Observations

Draw glacier diagram here.

Strategy Check

_____ Can you construct a model of a valley glacier?

_____ Can you correctly model and label the features left by a valley glacier?

Capillary Action

During a rain, some of the water that moves downward toward the water table and zone of saturation is trapped in tiny, hairlike openings. These openings are called capillaries. Capillaries store molecules of water until a dry period. Then some of the water returns to the surface. Plant roots get moisture from "dry" soil as the moisture moves from saturated soil up the capillaries to the surface.

Strategy

You will demonstrate how moisture moves from saturated soil into the capillaries of dry soil.

Materials

beaker (500-mL)
water
food coloring (red)
celery stalk with leaves
pencils (colored—green, red)

2 plastic drinking glasses (clear)
scissors
0.5 L sand (coarse)
pan

CAUTION: *Use care when handling sharp objects.*

Procedure

Part A

1. Fill the beaker half full of water and add a few drops of food coloring. Place the celery in the beaker. In the box labeled "Beginning" under Data and Observations, Part A, draw a diagram of the celery showing the color of the celery.

2. In the box labeled "After 2 days," diagram the celery after two days.

Part B

1. Cut the bottoms from the plastic glasses with scissors. Be careful not to crack the glasses.

2. Set the glasses upright in the pan. Fill each glass with sand.

3. Carefully pour water into one glass until the sand is saturated and some water flows into the pan.

4. Observe and diagram what happens to the water. Draw your diagram under Data and Observations, Part B.

Data and Observations

Part A

Beginning

After 2 Days

Laboratory Activity 1 (continued)

Part B

Questions and Conclusions

1. What happens in the glass of dry sand when the water reaches it?

_____

_____

2. Compare the action of the water in the sand with the action in the celery.

_____

_____

3. How do you know capillary action occurs in the celery?

_____

_____

4. How could capillary action occur in the desert?

_____

_____

5. What kind of rock would be best suited for capillary action?

_____

_____

Strategy Check

_____ Can you demonstrate capillary action in celery?

_____ Can you demonstrate capillary action in soil?

Carbon Dioxide and Limestone

Chapter 25

When carbon dioxide is dissolved in water, it forms a weak acid. This acid dissolves limestone. Many caves have deposits of limestone (calcite) in the form of stalactites and stalagmites. Calcite is also found as the cementing material in many sandstones and other limestones. Thus, limestone can be dissolved beneath the surface, and it can also be deposited beneath the surface.

Strategy

You will examine conditions under which carbon dioxide may be lost from a carbonated soft drink. You will observe the effect of the loss of carbon dioxide on the precipitation of calcium carbonate. You will compare these processes with the natural processes.

Materials

pan	ice cubes	plastic straw (flexible)
3 cans of carbonated	hammer	limewater ($Ca(OH)_2$ solution)
soft drinks	nail	beaker (100-mL)

Procedure

1. Place one can of carbonated drink in a pan of ice cubes and allow it to cool.
2. When the can is cool, shake it and one of the other cans gently.
3. Remove the top from each of the two cans while holding the cans over the pan or the sink. Record in Table 1 what occurs.
4. With the nail and hammer, make a small hole in the top of the third can. The hole should have about the same diameter as the straw.

5. Carefully slip the straw into the can. Hold the other end in the beaker filled with limewater. **CAUTION:** *Limewater may irritate the skin. Avoid contact.* Record your observations in Table 1.

Data and Observations

Table 1

Can	Observations
On ice	
Warm	
Limewater	

Laboratory Activity 2 (continued)

Questions and Conclusions

1. What gas is present in a carbonated drink?

_____

2. What happened when you removed the tops from two of the cans?

_____

Why?

_____

_____

3. Which soft drink lost its carbon dioxide faster?

_____

Why?

_____

_____

4. What process did you observe happening between the soft drink can with the straw and the limewater?

_____

_____

5. As the carbonic acid seeps through the roof of a cave, part of the water evaporates. What happens to the calcium carbonate?

_____

_____

_____

Strategy Check

_____ Can you determine the conditions under which carbon dioxide escapes from a soft drink?

_____ Can you observe the effect of the loss of carbon dioxide on the precipitation of calcium carbonate?

_____ Can you compare the processes observed here with natural processes?